D&S VOL. 15
FIRST NAVY JET TO SEE COMBAT

F9F Panther

in detail & scale

Bert Kinzey

Airlife Publishing Ltd.
England

Copyright 1993 by Detail & Scale, Inc. This book may not be reproduced in part or in whole without written permission from the publisher, except in the case of brief quotations used in reviews. Published in the United States by Kalmbach Publishing Company, 21027 Crossroads Circle, P.O. Box 1612, Waukesha, WI 53187.

CONTRIBUTORS:

Grumman Aerospace Corp.
National Archives
Lynn McDonnell
Gordon S. Williams
Alwyn T. Lloyd
U.S. Navy

Warren Munkasy
Col. Bob Williams
Ron Picciani
Combat Models
U.S. Marine Corps
Brian Baker

Detail & Scale, Inc. expresses a special thanks to Mr. H. J. "Schoney" Schonenberg and Mrs. Lois Lovisolo of the Grumman History Center for their untiring help, patience, and genuine friendliness displayed during the research conducted for this publication. A special thanks is also due Mr. William Shultz, also of Grumman, for his help.

Most photographs in this book are credited to their contributors. Photos with no credit were taken by the author.

Kinzey, Bert
  F9F Panther in detail & scale / by Bert Kinzey.
    p.   cm. -- (Detail & Scale series :   -v. 15)
  Originally published: Fallbrook, CA : Aero Publishers ; London : Arms and Armour Press, c1983.
  ISBN 0-89024-169-4 : $11.95
  1. Panther (Jet fighter plane) I. Title.
  II. Title: F9F Panther in detail and scale.
    UG1242.F5K52753   1993
    623.7'46044--dc20   93-10190
                                                          CIP

Front Cover: *An XF9F-2 is shown in its original neutral metal finish.*   **(Grumman)**

Rear Cover: *This unusual vertical color photo of an F9F-5 Panther shows the interior chromate green color in the partially open nose.*   **(Grumman)**

INTRODUCTION

This head-on view of the first XF9F-2 shows to good effect the simple clean lines of the Panther.(Grumman)

During WWII Grumman's F4F Wildcat and F6F Hellcat were regarded as simple, rugged, dependable, and efficient fighters. They were simple in design, which made them easy to mass produce and to maintain. They were simple to fly, so that large numbers of young college boys could be quickly taught to fly them in combat and on and off carrier decks. This allowed for a rapid expansion of Naval aviation in those early desperate days of the war. Their rugged dependable design brought many pilots back "home" across an unforgiving ocean after substantial battle damage had been received. Spectacular crashes aboard ship, that in some cases literally cut the aircraft in two, often resulted in little or no injury to the pilot. These first two "cats" earned Grumman a reputation that prompted one observer to say, "The name Grumman on an airplane is like the name Sterling on silver."

It is with this reputation that Grumman moved into the jet age shortly after WWII. The Panther story began in early 1946 when a four engine aircraft was proposed, but this proposal never got off of the drawing boards much less into the air. It was the availability of the British Rolls-Royce Nene engine that influenced the ultimate form that the Panther would take. With its 5,000 pounds of thrust, the Nene prompted Grumman to make a new proposal for a single engine day fighter. Ironically, the British also sold the Nene to the Soviets, and a Soviet version went into the MiG-15 Fagot, an aircraft that the Panther would meet in the skies over Korea. This resulted in jet fighters of completely different design, one American and one of Russian design, fighting each other while being powered by virtually the same engine.

This single engine day fighter was designated XF9F-2, and with the XF9F-3, the first Panthers took to the skies following the same simple, rugged, dependable tradition of the "cats" that had gone before.

On the pages that follow is the most detailed look at Grumman's first jet powered fighter ever published. Originally, this book was to include the F9F Cougar as well, but it proved totally impossible to cover both aircraft in only seventy-two pages. Therefore, we are releasing a companion volume to this one that covers the Cougar in detail. Many of the photographs were obtained through the help and excellent cooperation of Mr. H. J. "Schoney" Schonenberg and Mrs. Lois Lovisolo of Grumman's History Center. They made available scores of photographs that had never been published before and now appear in this publication for the first time. Special thanks is also due to Mr. Lynn McDonnell, formerly with Grumman, who spent much of his time assisting the author with this project.

DEVELOPMENTAL HISTORY

This fine study of the first XF9F-2 reveals the Panther's simple lines and clean appearance. The aircraft was polished to a mirror-like finish. (Grumman)

On June 1, 1945, Grumman Aircraft Corporation received an "outline specification for a high performance night fighter." This specification called for the design of a "side-by-side, two-seat, carrier-based, high-performance night fighter airplane." General requirements specified that the aircraft must be capable of making night intruder missions out to a radius of 350 miles, and must be able to attack both airborne and surface targets. Additionally, several of the more specific specifications are interesting to note. The maximum folded dimensions were not to exceed 46 feet in span, and 17 feet in height as dictated by available carrier elevator dimensions. Further, at least fifteen aircraft had to fit on a portion of a carrier's deck 96 feet wide and 200 feet long. The aircraft was required to have tricycle landing gear, and a preference was stated for at least two engines for reliability.

Crew requirements called for a pilot and radar operator in side-by-side seating, and the specification went on to state that, "...special consideration be given to their comfort." The two crew members had to be able to communicate directly, and the radar operator's visibility had to be as good as the pilot's.

For performance, the specification stated, "It must fly fast enough to catch the speediest of targets, and fly slow enough to stay behind the slowest type." It had to decelerate from 300 knots to 100 knots in fifteen seconds. Minimum top speed had to be at least 450 miles per hour at sea level, and 475 miles per hour at 20,000 feet. Climb requirements were 3,500 feet per minute at sea level and 2,500 feet per minute at altitude. These figures had to be obtained with full internal fuel, full armament, and all equipment. The structure had to be able to stand 5 gs with full internal load. The aircraft was further required to have at least four .60 caliber guns or 20mm cannon with a minimum of 250 rounds per gun. It had to be capable of carrying bombs, rockets, or parachute flare containers, although provisions for these were not required to be included in the original design proposal.

Interestingly enough, the choice of power plant was left to the contractor. It could be a reciprocating, turbojet, or gas turbine engine so long as it was produced or under development in the United States.

A "long range" radar, capable of detecting airborne targets at 10 to 20 miles, was required with 180 degrees coverage in azimuth, 60 degrees coverage up, and 30 degrees down being specified.

With these specifications to meet, Grumman issued a letter dated September 28, 1945, which included their proposal designated Design 75. In their opening remarks, Grumman expressed concern that the performance requirements of the aircraft with regard to speed and climb were too low. They stated that they had, "...developed a design possessing performance capabilities which are substantially in excess of the requirements..."

The proposed aircraft was a mid-wing, two-place night fighter approximately the size of the F7F Tigercat. It was to be powered by four Westinghouse 24C turbojet engines arranged in pairs under the wings. It

In this photo, the Panther poses with its contemporaries. These early Naval jet fighters include (top to bottom) the Vought Pirate, Grumman Panther, McDonnell Banshee, and Vought Cutlass. (National Archives)

Panthers were converted for the reconnaissance role as shown here. Details of photo Panthers are provided on pages 24 and 25, and on 46 and 47. (Grumman)

could be catapulted from carriers, or take-off unassisted from a clear deck. Total internal fuel capacity was 1,530 gallons, stored in three self-sealing cells. There was no provision for externally carried fuel tanks. Four 20mm cannon were to be carried with 250 rounds per gun. Two guns were to be located in each engine nacelle. Although not required, Grumman included provisions for spin-stabilized rockets. These would be carried internally in the nacelle fillets.

To decrease speed quickly as called for in the requirements, the rudder and bottom portion of the vertical tail below the horizontal stabilizer were designed to open like a split flap. When opened, they would act as effective speed brakes, creating drag over seven times that of the normal drag of the airplane. This speed brake was activiated by use of the pilot's brake pedals whenever the gear was retracted. Thus the pilot could "brake" the aircraft both in the air and on the ground by "stepping on the brakes" to activate the speed brake in the air or the normal brakes on the landing gear when the aircraft was on the ground. The "feel" of the brakes was to be the same both on the ground and in the air.

For storage on carriers, the wings folded in a rather conventional manner, and the aircraft also had a nose gear that would kneel down to allow the nose to be moved up under the tail or wings of another aircraft. This was a Grumman concept, and was tried on other aircraft such as the FJ-1 Fury.

The design met the +5 g and a -2.5 g requirement with safety wing tips. A combat weight of 23,000 pounds was stated. Performance was estimated at 608 miles per hour at sea level and 575 miles per hour at 25,000 feet. Rate of climb at sea level was 11,400 feet per minute, and 6,420 feet per minute at 20,000 feet. The design combat radius was 388 miles.

It must have looked like a promising design to the Navy, and it was given the designation XF9F-1, which stood for, F=fighter, 9=ninth type, F=Grumman's designator as contractor, -1=first model. However the project was soon cancelled on October 9, 1946. Meanwhile the Navy had already issued another set of specifications to Grumman, these being for a day fighter instead. In retrospect, it would appear that the requirements for the night fighter were met quite nicely by the Douglas F3D Skynight.

With the cancellation of the XF9F-1 project, Grumman turned its attention to Design 79. This was a series of four studies, "...to develop a naval fighter having combat performance exceeding that of current naval experimental fighters, and at the same time retaining the take-off and low speed performance of the F6F." Four studies, designated A through D, were made within the Design 79 program, and featured two aircraft with composite power plants, and two aircraft powered only with turbojet engines. Whichever design was chosen, the aircraft was to be operational within two years.

Study A was for an aircraft with an R2800-E reciprocating engine and a Derwent VI turbojet in the tail. The concept was not unlike the Ryan Fireball which actually was built.

Study B was similar to Study A except that the TG-100 prop-jet engine replaced the R2800-E while the Derwent VI turbojet remained the same.

Study C featured two Derwent VI engines in nacelles located in the wings. The design was not

Grumman's History Center has these two wood models that are significant in the development of the Panther. At left is design 75 for a four-engine two-seat night fighter that was designated XF9F-1. At right is design 79, Study C, which was the one most favored by Grumman, for a single-seat day fighter. It had two engines, and looked very much like the Gloster Meteor. However, it was the availability of the Rolls Royce Nene engine that was to lead to the single-engine day fighter that was to become the XF9F-2.

SPECIFICATIONS FOR DESIGN 79 STUDIES

CHARACTERISTICS	79-A	79-B	79-C	79-D
GENERAL				
Power Plant	R2800 + Derwent VI	TG-100 + Derwent VI	2 Derwent VI	1 Nene
Span	40'-8"	39'-10"	42'-5"	37'-0"
Span Folded	25'-7"	25'-3"	19'-6"	15'-5"
Length	37'-7"	39'-6"	40'-0"	38'-0"
Wing Area	322	311	362	276
Aspect Ratio	5.0	5.0	5.0	5.0
Taper Ratio	2.5:1	2.5:1	2.25:1	2.5:1
Wing Section	64.112	64.112	64.112	64.112
TAKE-OFF				
T.O. Gross Weight	14500	14000	16300	12400
Fuel Capacity (All Internal)	457	522	930	808
T.O. Wing Loading	45	45	45	45
T.O. Thrust Loading	1.16	1.14	2.04	2.18
T.O. Distance (25 Kt. Wind)	233	213	433	443
Average V/Cruise	275	325	350	375
Combat Radius	300	300	300	300
COMBAT				
Combat Gross Weight	13400	12800	14000	10500
Combat Wing Loading	41.6	41.2	38.7	38.1
Vmax.	548/15000	557/15000	598/S.L.	598/S.L.
Rate of Climb at Sea Level	7950	9170	10320	10550
Rate of Climb at 25,000 Feet	4850	5020	6350	6350
Design Load Factor	7.0	7.0	7.0	7.0
LANDING				
Landing Gross Weight	12000	11200	11600	8300
Landing Wing Loading	37.3	36.0	32.1	30.1
V/Stall Landing Condition	90	90	84	79
Armament (All aircraft)	Four 20 mm cannon with 800 rounds.			

DESIGN 79, STUDY A   **DESIGN 79, STUDY B**

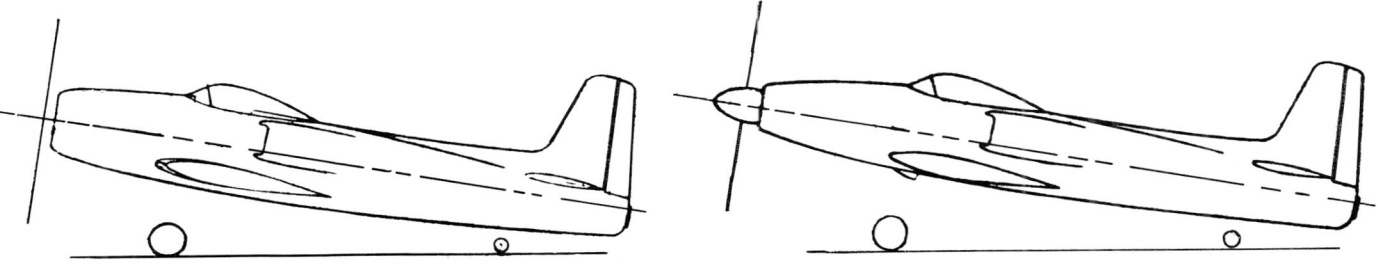

COURTESY OF GRUMMAN AEROSPACE CORP.

The F9F-5 was the later and more capable of the Panther series. **(Grumman)**

unlike the Gloster Meteor.

Study D was powered by a single Rolls Royce Nene engine. As with all studies, it was a straight wing, single seat day fighter armed with four 20mm cannon.

Grumman preferred Study C, and offered a strong case for the design. They claimed that it had, "...the advantage of ease of breakdown of components, both from a design and maintenance standpoint, and in addition had the recognized safety factor of twin engine reliability in flight." The two composite engined aircraft were not seriously considered since the emergence of the jet engine seemed to spell their obsolescence by the time the aircraft could be produced. Of the two, only the R2800-E design could be flying in the required two years. Grumman's conclusions also indicated that they did not believe the Nene-powered Study D could be ready in two years, probably because of the questionable availability of the engine.

But the Nene engine did become available, and seemingly was the class of the world's jet engines in its day. Thus the Navy opted for Study D with some modifications. The decision became official in June 1946, and Grumman was now committed to the development of the first flying prototypes for Design 79. The Navy called the design XF9F-2, even though it in no way decended from the XF9F-1 night fighter. Soon the name Panther was bestowed on the aircraft, thus following the tradition of naming Grumman's naval fighters after members of the cat family.

Three prototypes were ordered, 122475, 122476, and 122477, with the first and last becoming XF9F-2s and the second becoming the sole XF9F-3. It was identical to the -2s, except that it was powered by an Allison J33-A-8 engine instead of the Nene.

With no major changes being required, the F9F-2 and F9F-3 went into production, with the F9F-2 being produced in larger numbers. With several improvements, the "second generation" Panthers, the F9F-4 and F9F-5 followed the -2 and -3 into service with the -5 being the most produced of these two versions. The Navy adapted a number of F9F-2 airframes for use in the photographic reconnaissance role, and designated them F9F-2Ps. After finding these aircraft successful, they ordered thirty-six F9F-5Ps to be built as such by Grumman.

During its operational life, the F9F Panther made naval aviation history. It became the first Navy jet to enter combat, doing so with VF-51 on July 3, 1950, while operating off the USS Valley Forge, CV-45. It was the first Navy jet to down another jet, and delivered more ordnance against ground targets in Korea than any other jet aircraft. Out of a total of 826 jet fighters used in Korea by the U.S. Navy and Marines, no less than 715 were Panthers. Together they flew 78,000 combat missions, averaging about 110 missions each. Thus, while not the stellar air-to-air performer the F-86 was, the Navy and Marines got their money's worth with the Panther.

Almost before the first Panther prototypes flew, it was realized that the days of the straight wing jet fighter were numbered. Studies were begun to replace the Panther's straight wings with swept surfaces, and this proved to be quite successful. But that is the story of the F9F Cougar, and is covered in a companion volume on that aircraft. On the pages that follow, additional information is given on each version of the Panther, and numerous photographs and drawings show the aircraft in extensive detail.

PANTHER GENERAL ARRANGEMENT

COURTESY OF GRUMMAN AEROSPACE CORP.

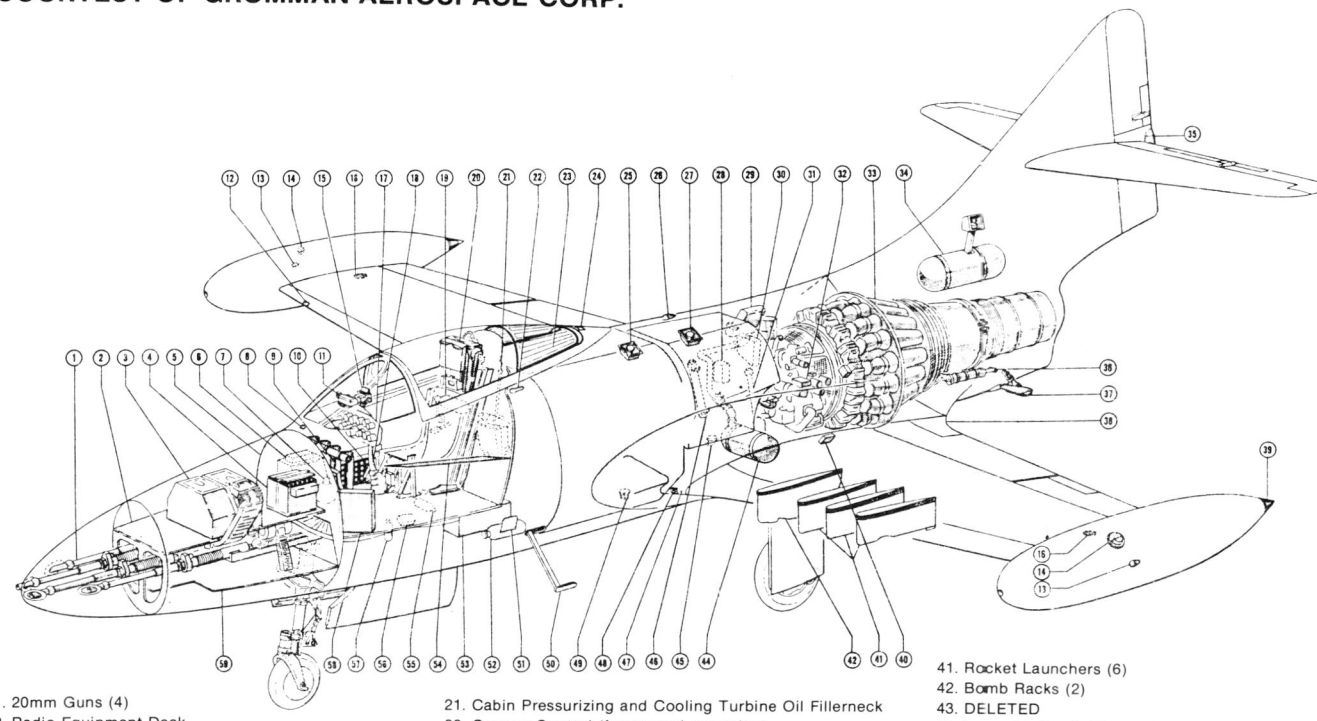

1. 20mm Guns (4)
2. Radio Equipment Deck
3. Inboard Guns Ammunition Boxes
4. Battery
5. Forward Armor Plate
6. Right Cockpit Distribution Box
7. Hydraulic System Accumulator
8. Barrier Guard
9. Rudder and Brake Pedals
10. Circuit Breaker Panel
11. Gun Camera
12. Auxiliary Wing Position Light
13. Wing Tip Position Lights
14. Wing Tip Tank Filler Cap
15. AFCS Gunsight
16. Formation Lights
17. Instrument Panel
18. Control Stick
19. Oxygen Bottle
20. Ejection Seat Face Cover Handles and Head Rest
21. Cabin Pressurizing and Cooling Turbine Oil Fillerneck
22. Canopy Control (for ground operation)
23. AN/ARN-6 Sense Antenna
24. Canopy Unlatch (for removal on ground)
25. Forward Fuel Tank Fillerneck
26. Top Fuselage Light
27. Rear Fuel Tank Fillerneck
28. Generator Connector Box
29. Upper Hydraulic Reservoir
30. Engine Junction Box
31. Engine Oil Fillerneck
32. Engine Accessories
33. Engine
34. Water Injection Fluid Tank
35. Tail Position Lights
36. Arresting Hook Recoil Strut
37. Tail Skid
38. Bomb Clearance Flap Door
39. Wing Tip Tank Dump Valve (2)
40. D-C External Power Receptacles
41. Rocket Launchers (6)
42. Bomb Racks (2)
43. DELETED
44. Lower Hydraulic Reservoir
45. Fuel Tank Water Drain
46. Aileron Booster Hydraulic Accumulator
47. Wing Lock Indicating Rod
48. Approach Light
49. Fuel System Drain Valve
50. Boarding Ladder
51. Handgrip and Step (ladder release)
52. Landing Gear Emergency Air Bottle
53. Outboard Guns Ammunition Boxes
54. Left Cockpit Console
55. Canopy Emergency Air Bottle
56. A-C External Power Receptacle
57. Brake and Seat Ejection Emergency Air Bottle
58. Left Cockpit Junction Box
59. Gun Deck

EJECTION SEAT

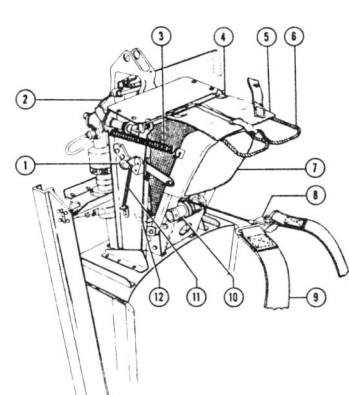
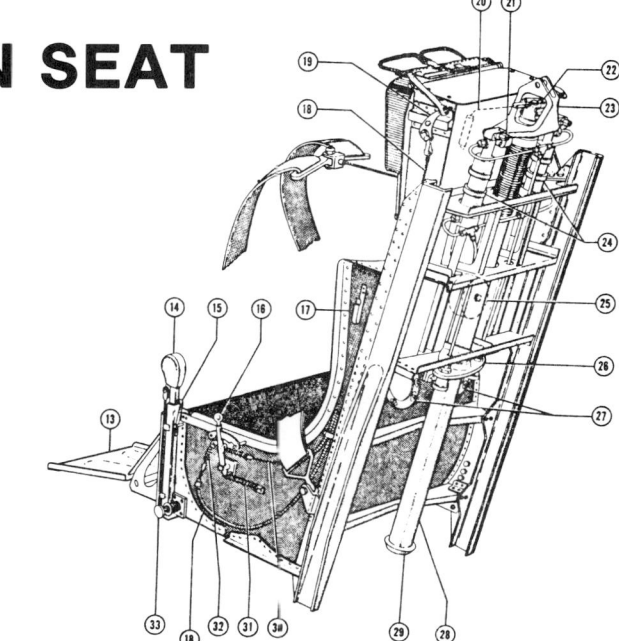

1. Headrest Adjusting Handle
2. Face Curtain-to-Firing Mechanism Cable
3. Headrest Positioning Spring
4. Face Curtain Hold-down Spring
5. Face Curtain (Partially extended)
6. Face Curtain Handles
7. Head Rest
8. Harness Attaching Fitting
9. Shoulder Harness
10. Harness Support Tube
11. Headrest Adjusting Handle Spring
12. Face Curtain Roller
13. Foot Rest Guide
14. Knee Brace
15. Knee Brace Uplock Spring
16. Harness Inertia Reel Lock-Unlock Control
17. Lap Belt Stowage Clip
18. Harness Inertia Reel Lock Emergency Cable
19. Harness Inertia Reel Emergency Control
20. Cable to Safety Pin
21. Trunnion Bolt
22. Firing Mechanism Fitting
23. Yoke Fitting
24. Seat Adjusting Cylinders
25. Harness Inertia Reel
26. Hydraulic Lines Fitting
27. Inspection Plates
28. Catapult Outer Cylinder
29. Hold-back Ring
30. Harness Inertia Reel Lock Cable
31. Harness Inertia Reel Control Return Spring
32. Harness Inertia Reel Lock Emergency Cable Tension Spring
33. Knee Brace Release Striker

WING FOLD DETAIL

Like most shipboard fighters, the Panther had folding wings. In this photo, the wings are shown at the angle to which the wings folded on production aircraft. (National Archives)

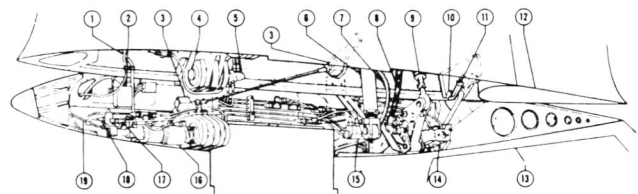

1. Electrical Cables
2. Electrical Junction Box
3. Aileron Tab Drive
4. Hinge Pin
5. Swivel - Wing Flap Cylinder and Droop Nose Cylinder Hydraulic Lines
6. Wing Folding Cylinder
7. Pitot Pressure Line (Right Wing Only)
8. Tip Tank Fuel Line
9. Aileron Push Rod
10. Rear Hinge Bolt
11. Wing Fold Timer Check Valve Stop
12. Outboard Wing Flap
13. Inboard Wing Flap
14. Wing Fold Timer Check Valve
15. Wing Foldling Cylinder Swivel
16. Wing Lock Cylinder
17. Wing Lock Control
18. Wing Lock Timer Check Valve
19. Wing Lock Indicator

Originally the Panther's wings were designed to fold to the vertical position as shown here. This was the same arrangement as on the Banshee. (Grumman)

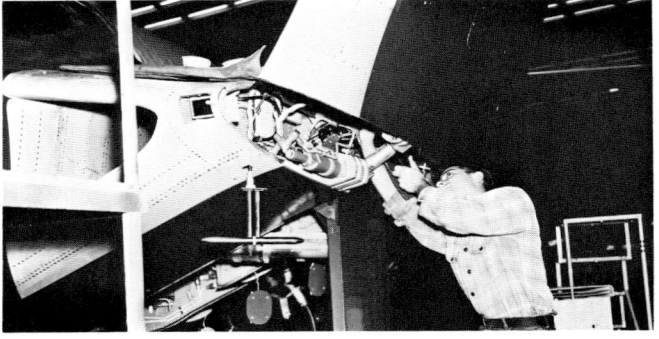

Here a mechanic works on the left wing fold mechanism, and many of the details are visible in this photo. (Grumman)

WING TIP TANKS

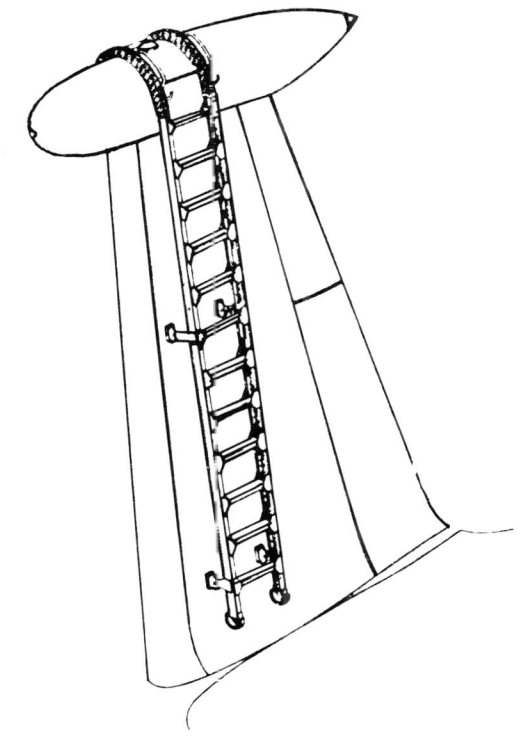

The wing tip fuel tanks on the Panther could be filled when the wings were folded. A ladder specially designed for this purpose was used. Included here are four photographs showing this device in use. At right is a drawing showing the details of the ladder. (Photos, U.S. Navy; Drawing, Courtesy of Grumman)

ENGINE DETAIL

Access to the engine on all Panthers was achieved by removing the tail section from the aircraft.
(National Archives)

COURTESY OF GRUMMAN AEROSPACE CORP.

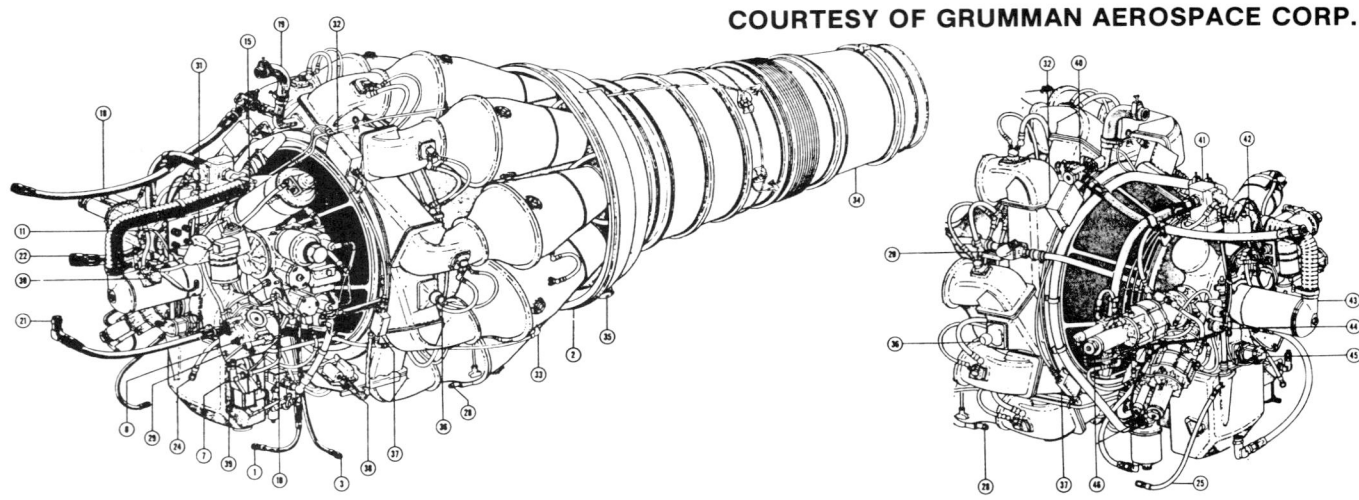

1. Drain Collector Tank Connection and Fuel System Drain Line
2. Engine Fireseal Baffle Assembly - 133225-1
3. Pressure Balancing Scupper and Engine-driven Fuel Booster Pump Vent Line
4. D-C External Power Receptacle Assembly - 134610-1
5. Tip Tank Fuel System Transfer Pump Installation - 132877
6. Engine Mount Clamp Fitting - 137587
6. Engine Mount Clamp Fitting - 137587 Washer - SP4300-9, Nut, Cotter
7. Hydraulic Pump Discharge Line and Pump Discharge Elbow
8. Hydraulic Pump Case Drain Line and Pump Case Drain Fitting
9. Generator D-C Output Cable (to "B" post on generator)
10. Engine Control Rod and Fuel Control Lever on Engine
11. Engine Electrical Cables and Receptacles
12. Booster Coil Relay Box Assembly - 134758-1.
12. Booster Coil Relay - AN3320-1.
12. Starter Undercurrent Relay - AN3391-1.
13. Water Injection Tank Fillerneck
14. Engine Connector Box Electrical Assembly - 134596
15. Starter Cables and Starter
16. Generator Cut-out Box Electrical Assembly - 134618
17. A-C Generator Cut-out Box Cable (to receptacle on generator)
18. Water Injection Shut-off Valve and Air Line to Engine
19. Cabin Pressurizing System Ducts
20. Water Injection System Fluid Line and Engine Inlet Connection
21. Hydraulic Reservoir Outlet Connection and Supply Line to Engine Pump
22. Fuel Supply Lines
23. Fuel System Main Shut-off Valve Installation - 132945
24. Hydraulic Seepage Pump Drain Lines
25. Engine Oil Sump Overboard Drain Elbow and Line
26. Tip Tank Fuel System Selector Valve Installation - 132878
27. Lower Engine Mount Rod and Bottom Engine Suspension Bracket
28. Combustion Chamber Drain Lines and Fittings
29. Engine-Driven Hydraulic Pump
30. Radio Noise Filter Capacitor Assembly - 134688-2 (4 mid - 50 volt dc)
31. Oil Sump Fillerneck Assembly - 133150
32. Ignition Exciter Unit
33. Igniter Plub
34. Flexible Tailpipe Assembly - 133240
35. Cooling Air Outlet Connection - 133207 Clamp
36. Engine Suspension Trunnion
37. Compositor
38. Fuel Pressure Warning Switches Installation - 133019
39. Fuel Shut-off Actuating Mechanism Installation - 133048
40. Water Injection System Pressure Regulating Valve
41. Engine-Driven Fuel Booster Pump
42. Fuel and Oil Pressure Transmitter Installation - 133167
42. Fuel Pressure Transmitter
42. Oil Pressure Transmitter
43. Generator
43. Cooling Air Tube Installation - 133160
44. Fuel Pressure Warning Switch Installation - 133155
45. Tachometer Generator R88-G-1320-50
46. Top and Bottom Fuel Pumps

Aircraft shown with tail section removed. (National Archives)

Close-up of left side of the engine showing the relative simplicity as compared with today's engines.
(National Archives)

LANDING GEAR

![Panther head-on view]

This head-on view shows the Panther's tricycle landing gear to good effect. Tie-down cables are also visible.
(Grumman)

The nose gear detail is clearly shown in this photograph. Also note the perforated speed brake just aft of the nose gear doors. (National Archives)

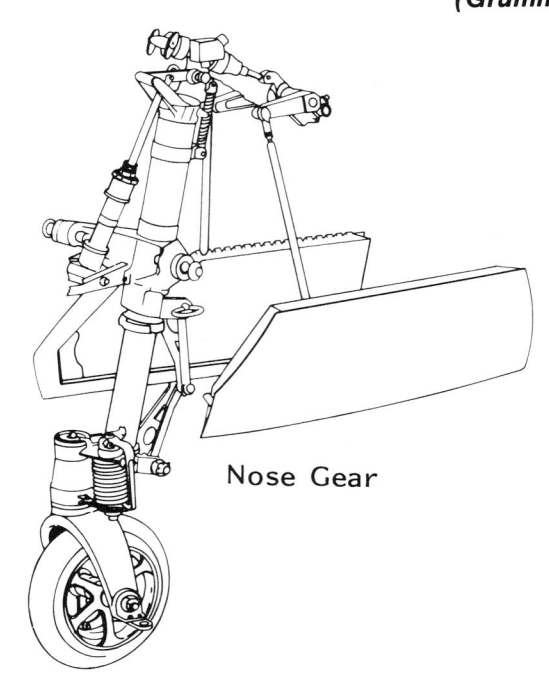

Nose Gear

In this photograph, both the inside and outside main wheel detail can be studied. Also note the extended boarding step. *(Grumman)*

This photo shows the strut actuating cylinder and interior of the gear well. Note that the inner main gear was usually closed when the aircraft was on the ground. The interior of the wells were chromate green. *(Grumman)*

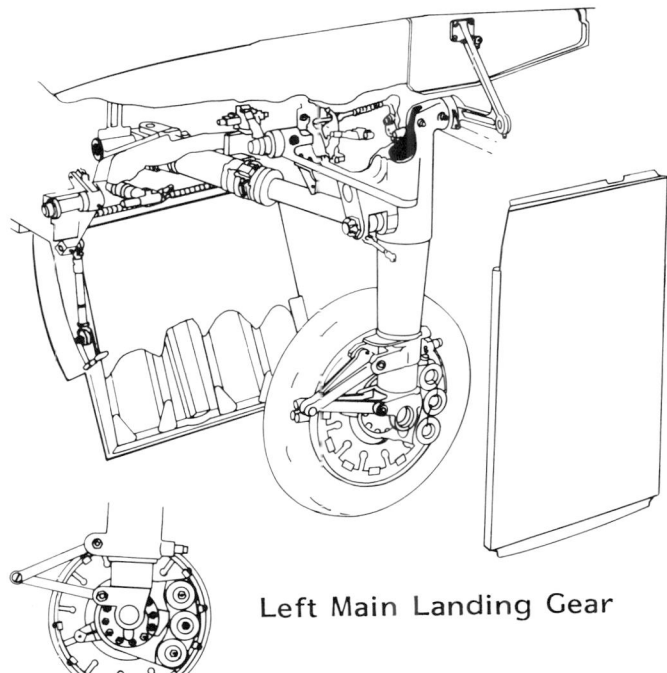

Left Main Landing Gear

UNDERSIDE DETAILS

This underside view of a Panther that ran off the end of a runway affords a great view of the gear wells, struts, and inner flap wells. *(Grumman)*

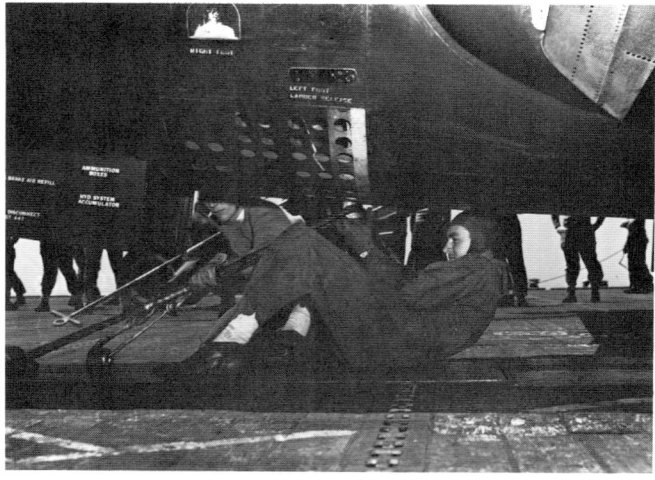

Here deck crewmen attach the catapult bridle to a Panther. The perforated speed brake is clearly visible here. *(National Archives)*

Panthers had a tail skid at the extreme rear of the fuselage. Also note the tail hook and its housing. *(Grumman)*

NOSE ACCESS

The Panther featured a nose section that could be pulled forward on rails, or removed entirely for access to the cannon and other equipment.

Above left: Nose section right side in the closed position. *(Grumman)*

Above right: Right side with nose section pulled forward on the rails. *(Grumman)*

Right: Drawing showing how the nose section was moved forward on the rails. *(Grumman)*

Below left: Left side of nose with nose section pulled forward on the rails. *(Grumman)*

Below right: Left side view with nose section completely removed from the aircraft. *(Grumman)*

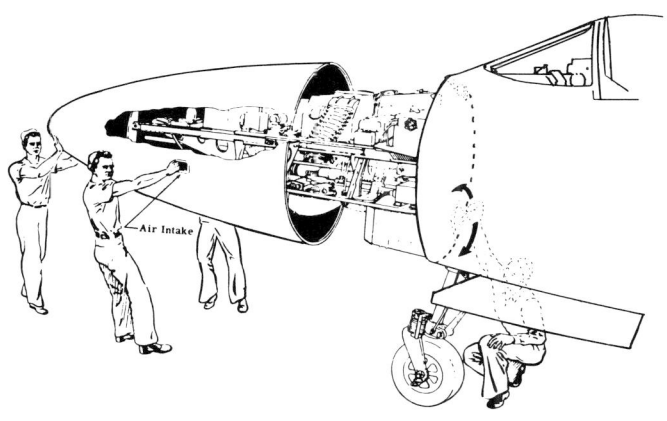

F9F-2

This photo of an XF9F-2 shows the nose boom and a second probe on the vertical tail. Also clearly visible is the Panther logo on the nose. *(Grumman)*

After cancellation of the XF9F-1 night fighter project, Grumman turned its full attention to Design 79. Although they had preferred the two-engine Study C design, the Navy wanted the single-engine Nene powered aircraft, and that is where developmental work began. The nose was lengthened, and the area around the tail pipe was enlarged. Otherwise, the design proceeded with very little in the way of changes. Then, in November 1947, the first XF9F-2 Panther rolled out from Grumman's plant at Bethpage, New York. The first flight was made by "Corky" Meyer on November 24, only seventeen months after the initial studies for Design 79 had begun. The other XF9F-2 prototype soon joined the first in flight testing.

Originally there were no tip tanks on the Panther, but these were soon fitted, and not only added 120 gallons each to the fuel capacity, but also improved aileron response. Although these tanks were detachable, they could not be jettisoned in flight. Valves at the trailing end of the tanks allowed quick venting of the fuel to lighten the load while in flight. Once fitted, Panthers were seldom seen without these tanks.

Ram-jet engines, and also rockets, were proposed for use on the wing tips in place of the tanks. The ram-jets were only effective at low altitude, and were envisioned as aids to boost climb rate after take-off. The rockets, with a short burn duration, were proposed for the same purpose. Neither design was ever used, and it does not take much imagination to visualize what would have happened if only one ram-jet or rocket had fired at low altitude.

Flight testing of the XF9F-2 lasted for quite some time, and was marred by the loss of one of the prototypes on October 28, 1948. It was soon replaced by an early production F9F-2. As produced, F9F-2s had an empty weight of 9,303 pounds, and a maximum gross weight of 19,500 pounds. An internal fuel load of 923 gallons was carried, and provided a range in excess of 1,100 miles. Top speed was around 525 miles per hour, and it could climb to 10,000 feet in less than seventy seconds. To aid in carrier landings, it had leading edge flaps on the wings, which was a new feature. These devices helped lower the landing speed of the aircraft.

In this view from above and behind, the auxilliary air intake blow-in doors are visible. They were larger on the XF9F-2 than on the production aircraft. *(Grumman)*

Shown here in flight, two early F9F-2s fly in formation. Wing tanks are yet to be added. Again note the blow-in doors on the fuselage. (Williams via Lloyd)

It was the British Nene engine that prompted the Navy to chose the Study D design, but the engines that went into production F9F-2s were not British built. They were built under license in the United States by Pratt & Whitney, and designated J42-P-6. It produced 5,000 pounds of thrust dry, and 5,700 pounds of thrust wet. However, it had no afterburner.

The first production F9F-2 made its maiden flight on November 24, 1948, exactly one year after the first flight by and XF9F-2. It was followed by 566 more examples before production gave way to the later versions. During this time there were two notable changes made to these initial Panthers. First was the conversion of a number of -2s to photographic reconnaissance aircraft, which is covered on pages 24 and 25, and second was the F9F-2B modification. This later modification involved the addition of a Mark 51 bomb rack under the inboard portion of each wing. A 1,000 pound bomb could be carried on each. This was in addition to the six standard racks used for carrying rockets and smaller bombs. But as the Mark 51 rack was retrofitted to all -2s, the "B" designator was dropped. A look at Panther armament and ordnance begins on page 52. Later in life, F9F-2s were also converted to F9F-2D drones and F9F-2DK drone directors.

F9F-2 PANTHER PRODUCTION

XF9F-2	122475 and 122477
F9F-2	122563, 122567, 125669
	122570, 122572
	122586 thru 122589
	123016 thru 123019
	123044 thru 123067
	123077 thru 123086
	123397 thru 123713
	125083 thru 125155
	127086 thru 127215

TOTALS: XF9F-2 2
F9F-2 567

These two views show F9F-2, 122567, which was tested with air scoops in place of the standard blow-in doors. The idea never got past the test stage. (Grumman)

This F9F-2 has an unusual paint scheme in that the upper surfaces are the standard blue, but the lower surfaces are painted gray. (Grumman)

Several F9F-2s were designated F9F-2Bs after being fitted with a fourth pylon on each wing. These pylons allowed the aircraft to carry 1,000 pound bombs, external fuel tanks, and other ordnance. But when earlier F9F-2s were retrofitted with this feature, the "B" suffix was dropped. (via Munkasy)

F9F-2s were used extensively in Korea. Here, Lt(jg) Leonard Gordinier, USNR, pilots his Panther on a strike over the Hamhung rail center. The aircraft is from VF-721 operating off of the USS Boxer, CV-21. The nose flash and tail tip are red. This photo was taken in June 1951. (U.S. Navy)

Panthers are being launched from the USS Valley Forge for a strike over Korea. (Grumman)

Panthers are shown here with one of the Navy's other workhorses in Korea, the F4U Corsair. Visible in the center of the photo is a Skyraider. These three types of aircraft provided most of the Navy's punch against targets in Korea. (Grumman)

F9F-2s from VF-191 are shown with an F9F-2P returning from a reconnaissance mission over Korea. The carrier is the USS Princeton. (Grumman)

F9F-2 COCKPIT DETAIL

These two photos show two variations of instrument panels used in the F9F-2. The lower instrument panel is the later style, and note that the compass at lower center has a swept wing aircraft design on it.   (Grumman)

Left console showing "stepped" configuration and throttle. (Grumman)

Right console showing wing folding control, radios, lighting, and cabin environment controls. Also note the circuit breaker panel. (Grumman)

23

F9F-2P

VC-61 operated F9F-2Ps on several carriers during the Korean conflict. Here two photo Panthers fly over the USS Boxer, CV-21. *(National Archives)*

The Navy realized a need for a new photo reconnaissance aircraft with the performance of its new jet fighters. The solution was accomplished by removing the guns from an F9F-2, and replacing them with cameras and the necessary windows in the nose of the aircraft. A viewfinder replaced the gunsight in the cockpit, and camera controls were placed on the left console. Camera windows were cut in the bottom of the nose and on each side. Access to the camera bay was through a hatch on top of the nose. The nose section was not lengthened for this conversion, thus the dimensions remained the same as for the standard -2.

In Korea, most of these aircraft, designated F9F-2P, served with VC-61, and were assigned to carriers in various detachments. A relatively few photo Banshees also served with VC-61, but the lion's share of the work was done by the Panthers. Being unarmed, they were escorted to and from the target areas by the gun-carrying Panthers from the carrier's fighter squadrons. VC-61 aircraft were usually identifiable by the PP code painted on their tails.

An F9F-2P over Korea. Note the mission markings on the nose. *(Grumman)*

Two F9F-2s escort an F9F-2P from VC-61 over the rugged Korean countryside in 1952. *(Grumman)*

View looking down into the camera bay of an F9F-2P. (Grumman)

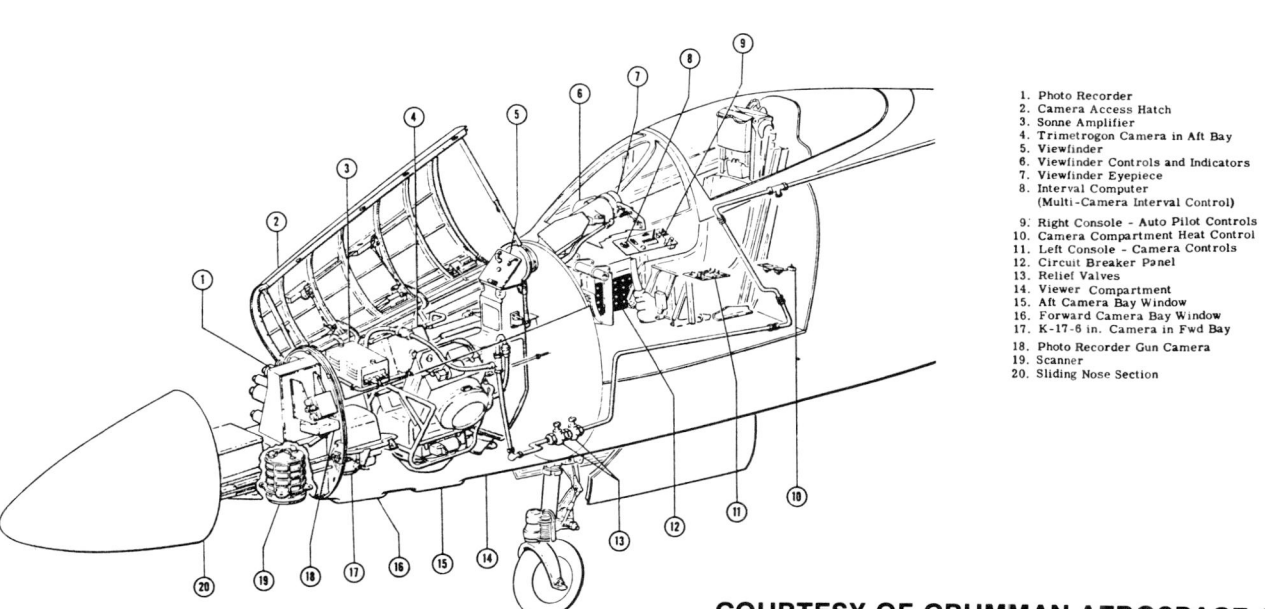

1. Photo Recorder
2. Camera Access Hatch
3. Sonne Amplifier
4. Trimetrogon Camera in Aft Bay
5. Viewfinder
6. Viewfinder Controls and Indicators
7. Viewfinder Eyepiece
8. Interval Computer (Multi-Camera Interval Control)
9. Right Console - Auto Pilot Controls
10. Camera Compartment Heat Control
11. Left Console - Camera Controls
12. Circuit Breaker Panel
13. Relief Valves
14. Viewer Compartment
15. Aft Camera Bay Window
16. Forward Camera Bay Window
17. K-17-6 in. Camera in Fwd Bay
18. Photo Recorder Gun Camera
19. Scanner
20. Sliding Nose Section

COURTESY OF GRUMMAN AEROSPACE CORP.

The XF9F-3 is shown here with one wing folded and one extended. Tip tanks are fitted as is a nose boom. The Panther logo and the word "Panther" are blue outlined in red. (Grumman)

F9F-3

The concept of the XF9F-3 was developed concurrently with the XF9F-2, while the development of the actual aircraft ran about nine months behind the XF9F-2 program. The first flight of the sole prototype was on August 16, 1948, and as with the XF9F-2 prototypes, there were no serious problems encountered.

The XF9F-3 was essentially the same as the XF9F-2 except that it was powered by an Allison J33-A-8 engine that produced 4,600 pounds of thrust as compared to 5,000 pounds with the Nene or J42-P-6. The rationale for the development of a version with a different engine was simple. Jet engines were still in their infancy, and the use of a British engine, license-produced in the United States, could lead to unforeseen problems in reliability or availability, and thus leave the aircraft without an engine. Therefore it seemed prudent to develop a version using the best available U.S. engine, even though it was inferior to the British engine. Accordingly, the performance of the F9F-3 was less than that of the -2, but the Navy had its back-up---just in case.

After the prototype, fifty-four examples of the F9F-3 were produced. But things did work out well for the British engine, and most of the these aircraft were brought up to -2 standards by retrofitting them with the J42-P-6 engine. Although the F9F-3 got into the air after the F9F-2, it was the F9F-3 that first entered squadron service on May 8, 1949 with VF-51.

F9F-3 PANTHER PRODUCTION

XF9F-3	122476
F9F-3	122560 thru 122562
	122564 thru 122566
	122568 thru 122571
	122573 thru 122585
	123020 thru 123043
	123068 thru 123076

TOTALS: XF9F-3 1
F9F-3 54

A good head-on view of the XF9F-3 reveals markings for the yaw string painted on the anti-glare panel. (Grumman)

The second production F9F-3 is shown here in the standard overall blue scheme, but no tip tanks are installed on the wing. (Grumman)

EMERSON TURRET AIRCRAFT

F9F-3, 122562, was tested with an Emerson turret installed. Four .50 caliber machine guns replaced the standard 20 mm cannon. These guns could be angled in excess of ninety degrees within the turret, and the turret itself could be rotated so that the guns could be pointed in any direction in a 360 degree arc around the aircraft centerline. *(Grumman)*

This close-up view shows the guns displaced about ninety degrees, and the turret rotated slightly to the right. *(Grumman)*

These three in-flight views show the guns and turret in various firing positions. The turret was never used on production aircraft.
(Grumman)

F9F-2/3 DIMENSIONS

DIMENSION	ACTUAL	1/72nd SCALE	1/48th SCALE	1/32nd SCALE
Wingspan (Extended)	37' 11.88"	6.33"	9.50"	14.25"
Wingspan (Folded)	23' 5"	3.90"	5.85"	8.78"
Length (Normal)	37' 11.31"	6.32"	9.49"	14.29"
Length (Nose Extended)	41' 3.31"	6.88"	10.32"	15.48"
Tail Span	17' 2.5"	2.87"	4.30"	6.45"
Height (To Top of Tail)	11' 4"	1.89"	2.83"	4.25"
Height (To Top of Folded Wing)	16' 9"	2.79"	4.19"	6.28"
Wheel Track	11' 7"	1.93"	2.90"	4.34"
Wheel Tread	8' 3"	1.38"	2.06"	3.09"

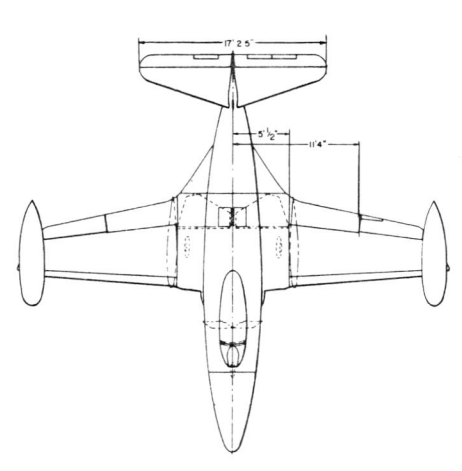
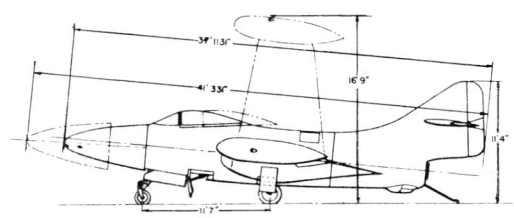
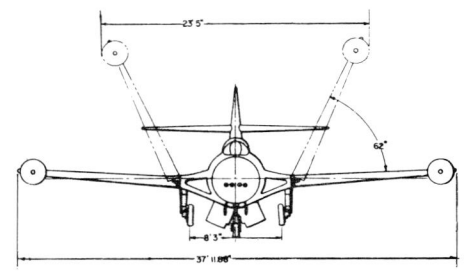

Five-view drawings of the F9F-2 & 3 Panther and many other aircraft are available separately in 1/48th scale at a nominal price. Write to Aero Publishers, Inc., 329 West Aviation Road, Fallbrook, California, 92028, for details.

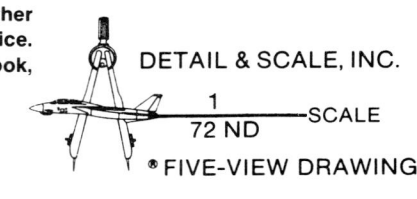

DETAIL & SCALE, INC.
$\frac{1}{72\text{ ND}}$ SCALE
® FIVE-VIEW DRAWING

F9F-2/3 PANTHER

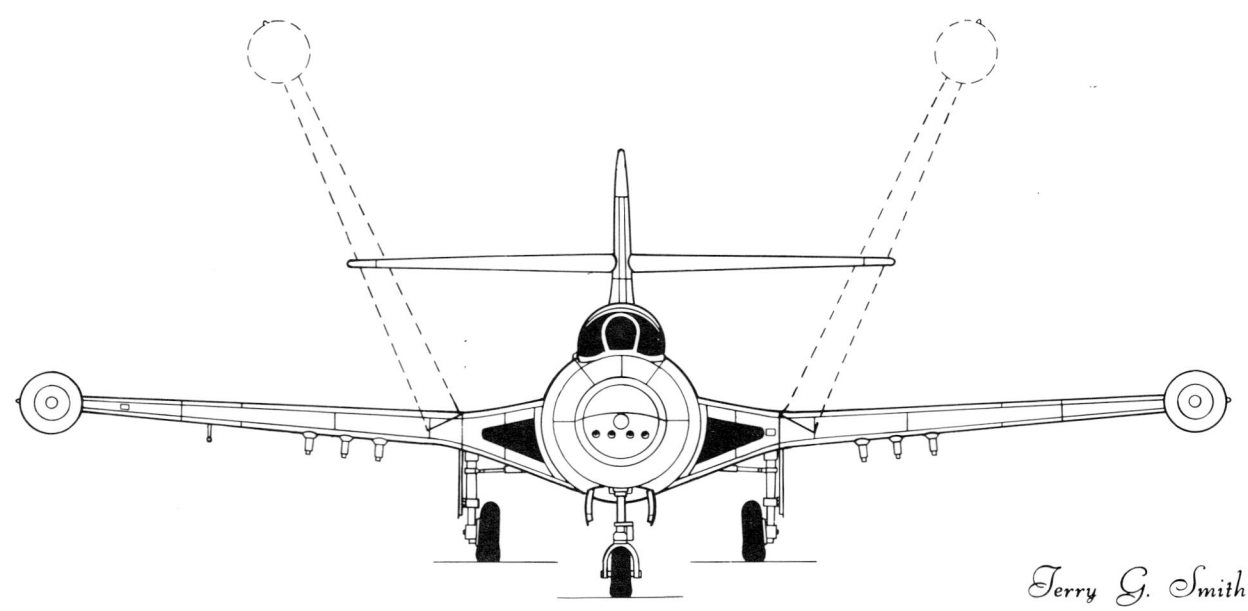

Jerry G. Smith

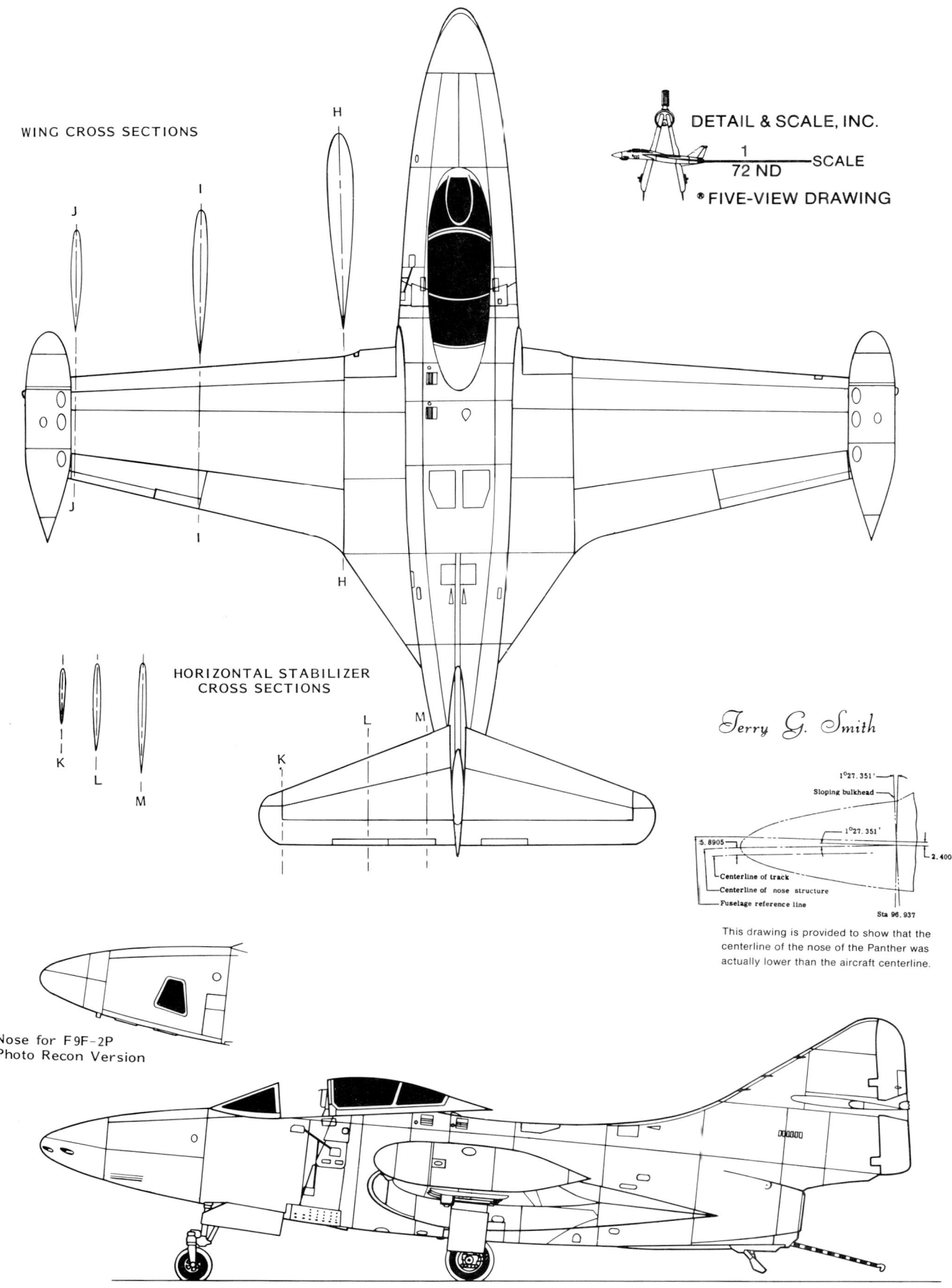

WING CROSS SECTIONS

HORIZONTAL STABILIZER CROSS SECTIONS

DETAIL & SCALE, INC.
1/72ND SCALE
® FIVE-VIEW DRAWING

Jerry G. Smith

This drawing is provided to show that the centerline of the nose of the Panther was actually lower than the aircraft centerline.

Nose for F9F-2P Photo Recon Version

31

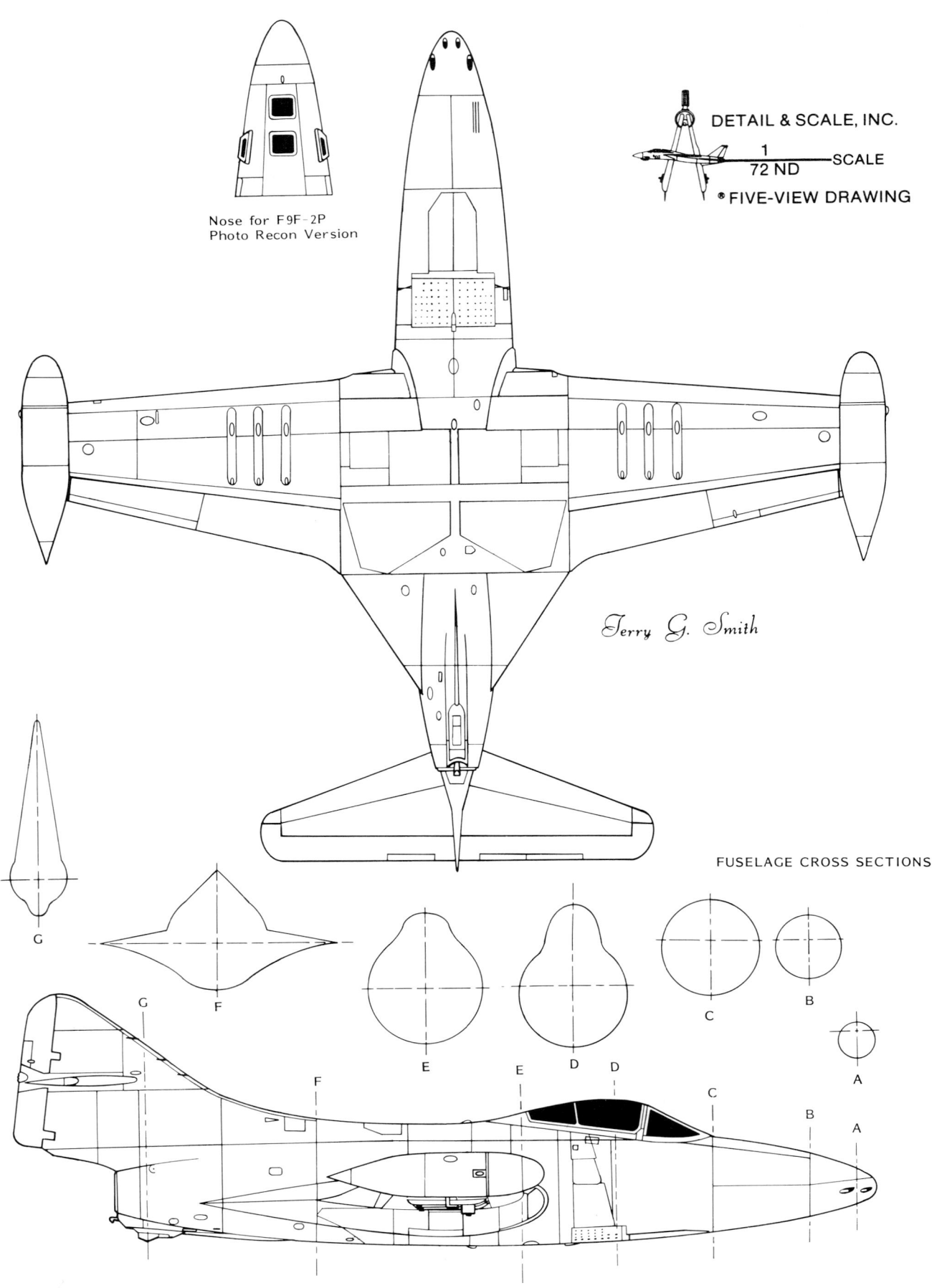

COLOR GALLERY

The second XF9F-2 is shown here in flight after tip tanks were added. The panther on the nose is dark blue outlined in red, as is the name "Panther" below it. (Grumman)

The first F9F-3, 122560, is shown here with six five-inch rockets under its wings. The red and white colors on the rockets were not standard. Rockets used in combat were usually a dull silver color with an olive drab warhead. (Grumman)

F9F-4

An F9F-4 is displayed for public viewing in June 1951. Note the modified intakes and taller tail as compared to the earlier F9F-2 and -3. A red FOD cover is placed in the intake, and the yaw string can be seen hanging down just ahead of the nose number. *(Grumman)*

F9F-4, 125919, of VMA-334 is shown with a colorful red flame design on its nose and tip tanks. This squadron was deactivated in 1955. *(Leader Collection)*

An F9F-2 from VF-123 shows its yellow bands with blue stars on the rudder and tip tanks.
(Williams via Munkasy)

This close-up of another VF-123 Panther reveals that the small wing fences have been retro-fitted to this aircraft.
(Williams via Munkasy)

MARINE PANTHERS

This unusual photo shows a Marine Panther mounted on jacks for maintenance. (Williams via Munkasy)

This Panther, an F9F-5, 125577, is shown in the later gray over white scheme. The aircraft is from VMA-223. (Picciani)

F9F-5P

An F9F-5P, 126278, from VMJ-3 poses with red and white markings. (Leader Collection)

This in-flight view of another VMJ-3 F9F-5P is included to show how the red design appears on both sides of the tip tanks. (Picciani)

A wingman in an F9F-2 is seen here from his leader's cockpit. Note the lack of the usual aluminum colored leading edges on the wings. (Williams via Munkasy)

These VMF-311 Panthers are waiting to be loaded with bombs prior to a mission against targets in Korea. (Williams via Munkasy)

A long line of 500 pound bombs is positioned in front of VMF-311 aircraft. Marine Panthers delivered thousands of tons of ordnance against Korean targets, but seldom got the publicity received by the shipboard aircraft. (Williams via Munkasy)

VMF-115

A VMF-115 Panther taxis past two others at a Korean base. (Williams via Munkasy)

Crewmen are removing the tail section of this VMF-115 F9F-5 prior to servicing the jet engine.
(Williams via Munkasy)

Bombs are being loaded on this Panther. Note the bomb trolley under the left wing.
(Williams via Munkasy)

An F9F-2 of VMF-115 is shown parked on Marston matting in Korea during 1952. (Picciani)

A VMF-115 F9F-5 has one 1,000 pound and two 250 pound bombs under each wing.
(Williams via Munkasy)

39

These two photographs show F9F-2 Panthers from VF-31 on board the USS Leyte, CV-32. VF-31 flew missions over Korea off of the Leyte from October 1950 through January 1951. *(Grumman)*

The F9F-4 featured several physical changes from the earlier Panthers while sharing a common airframe with the F9F-5. The most noticeable change was the taller, more pointed, tail. Less noticeable was the longer fuselage caused by an insertion of a plug just forward of the wing roots. *(Grumman)*

F9F-4

The F9F-4 was the most unsuccessful of the Panther series, yet it could have been the most capable performer. It was the Allison J33-A-16 engine with 6,950 pounds of thrust (using water injection), that delivered the increase in performance, but it also was the cause of the problems that resulted in many of the F9F-4s being re-engined with the J48-P-6/8 used in the F9F-5. This completed the irony begun with the F9F-3, where the back-up or alternate engine source proved more of a problem than the British designed engine.

The F9F-4 had a range of 1,175 miles and a ceiling of 44,600 feet. It weighed 10,042 pounds empty, which was just over 100 pounds less than the -5 with which it shared a common airframe. This "second generation" airframe had a taller tail, lengthened fuselage, and revised air intakes. These new features are covered in more detail in the section on the F9F-5 beginning on the next page. It could carry an external load of 4,000 pounds, which was considerably more than the 2,800 pounds usually considered tops for the F9F-2.

But the Allison engine was plagued by bearing failures, and never was totally suitable. Initially the engine problems delayed the first flight of the first F9F-4 until July 6, 1950, which was over six months after the first F9F-5 first flew. Most -4s were assigned to the Marine Corps, and some were used in Korea from land bases.

F9F-4 PANTHER PRODUCTION

XF9F-4	123084*
F9F-4	125081
	125156 thru 125227
	125913 thru 125948
TOTALS: XF9F-4	1
F9F-4	109

*The XF9F-4 was converted from an existing F9F-2 airframe.

F9F-5

The F9F-5 became the standard production aircraft of the later Panther series. This Panther carries a non-standard in-flight refueling probe like those later fitted to Cougars. The new shape to the intakes is visible in this photo, but the small wing fences have not been added. (Grumman)

The F9F-5 was the last of the four versions of the Panther that were produced, and it was built in greater quantities than any other version. It was the last step in straight wing naval fighters before swept surfaces made their appearance permitting carrier aviation to keep pace with the land-based aircraft that were beginning to fly past the sound barrier.

Powered with an uprated Pratt & Whitney J48-P-6 or -8, which was based on the British Tay engine, the F9F-5 had 7,000 pounds of thrust with water/alcohol injection, and 6,250 pounds maximum dry thrust. Its top speed was 604 miles per hour at sea level at combat weight. Rate of climb was about 6,000 feet per minute, and it had a range of 1,300 miles and a ceiling of 42,800 feet. Empty weight was 10,147 pounds, basic weight was 11,013 pounds, and combat weight was 15,359 pounds. Maximum take-off weight from land was 21,245 pounds, and 20,600 pounds was the maximum carrier take-off weight.

The F9F-5, along with the F9F-4, were in the "sec-

This -5 from VF-111 shows the small wing fence just outboard of the intake. (National Archives)

ond generation" Panthers, and included some notable changes over the earlier F9F-2 and -3. The vertical tail was taller and more pointed at the tip. This change was an attempt to solve the directional stability problems that plagued the Panther throughout its career. The fuselage was lengthened just ahead of the wing root in order to provide more fuel for the J48 engine which had a higher fuel consumption than the earlier J42. This lengthening of the fuselage also contributed to the need for a taller tail. Another new feature was the reshaped air intakes that came to a point at the outboard point where the leading edge of the wing began. Although not originally fitted, a small wing fence was later added just outboard of the intake openings. This fence was subsequently added to older Panthers still in service. See page 45 for detailed look at this feature.

Armament remained four 20mm cannon with 190 rounds per gun. Two 1,000 pound bombs could be carried or up to six 500 pound bombs. Other combinations included eight 250 pound bombs, eight 100 pound bombs, on six 5 inch rockets.

The first flight of an F9F-5 was made on December 21, 1949, with the first delivery being made on November 5, 1950. Production continued through January 13, 1953, during which time 616 were built. In addition to these, many F9F-4s were fitted with the J48 engine and brought up to -5 standards.

Right: Late in their operational life, some Panthers wore the light gull gray over white scheme. Also visible under the noses of aircraft 56 and 39 is the AN/ARA-25 adapter fairing like the ones used later on many Cougars. **(Grumman)**

Below: This F9F-5, in an unusual natural metal scheme, is being hoisted aboard its carrier. In the background, other Panthers in the standard blue scheme await their turn. **(National Archives)**

The wheel chocks of this F9F-5 are being removed after the aircraft has been brought up to the flight deck in preparation for a flight. (National Archives)

F9F-5 PANTHER PRODUCTION

XF9F-5	123085*
F9F-5	125080 and 125082
	125228 thru 125313
	125447 thru 125476
	125489 thru 125499
	125533 thru 125648
	126627 thru 126672
	125893 thru 125912
	125949 thru 126256

TOTALS: XF9F-5 1
F9F-5 616

*The XF9F-5 was converted from an existing F9F-2 airframe.

F9F-5 COCKPIT DETAIL

Instrument panel detail in an F9F-5. (Grumman)

Left console detail in an F9F-5. Note that the consoles in the -5 do not have the stepped configuration used on the -2. (Grumman)

Right console detail. (Grumman)

WING DETAILS

One of the major changes to the later Panthers involved the air intakes. This view shows the small wing fence that was added just outboard of the intakes. Although not originally on the first -5s, it soon became standard. It was also retrofitted to some F9F-2s. (Grumman)

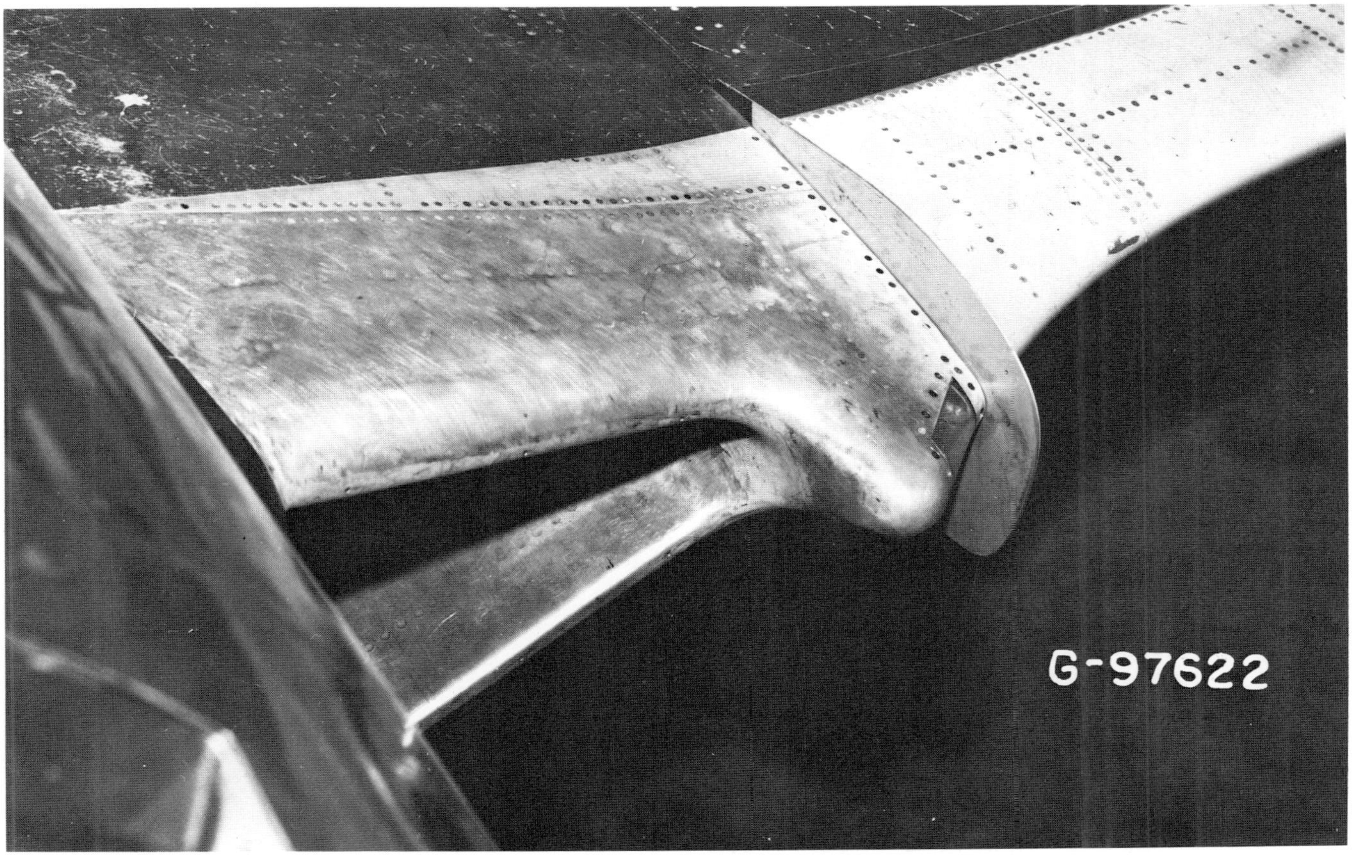

This top view shows how the intake's leading edge was reshaped. The wing fence is again visible. (Grumman)

F9F-5P

Like the earlier -2, thirty-six F9F-5Ps were built as photo recon versions. The arrangement was basically the same as on the F9F-2P, although the nose was longer. (Grumman)

With the success experienced with the F9F-2P conversion, the Navy ordered thirty-six F9F-5Ps built as such from the start by Grumman. These aircraft had the taller tail, stretched fuselage, wing fence, revised intakes, and J48 engine of the standard -5s. Additionally, it had the General Electric G-3 autopilot installed for use when the cameras were rolling.

Unlike the -2P, the nose section of the -5P was lengthened about twelve inches to accommodate the cameras. The cameras could perform photographic mapping as well as the usual photographic reconnaissance mission. Later, the same arrangement would be used in the F9F-6P Cougar.

No rocket racks were carried by the -5P, but inboard pylons were wet and could carry two 150 gallon fuel tanks to extend range. Performance of the -5P was virtually the same as the standard F9F-5.

F9F-5P PANTHER PRODUCTION

F9F-5P   125314 thru 125321
                              126265 thru 126290
                              127471 thru 127472
           TOTAL: 36 Aircraft

This view of an F9F-5P shows the vertical camera windows under the nose and the right side camera to good effect. (Grumman)

The forward portion of the nose on photographic Panthers slid forward as shown here. (National Archives)

Looking down into the camera nose with the cameras removed. *(Grumman)*

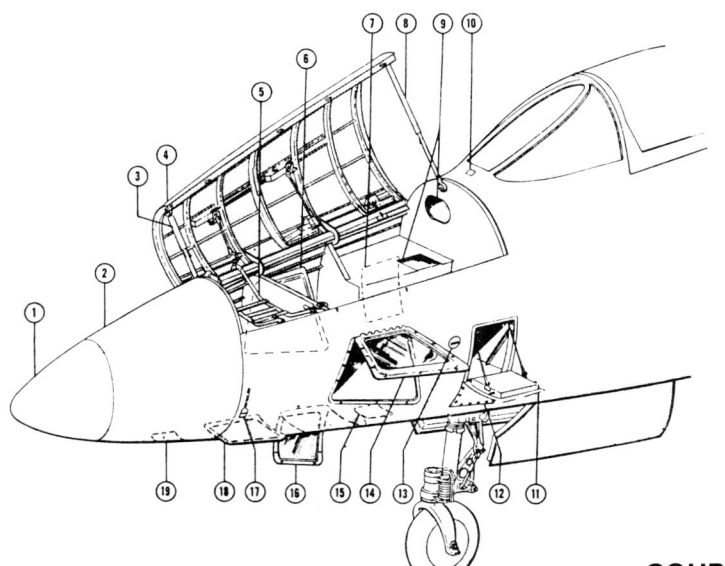

1. Plastic Nose Cap
2. Sliding Nose Section
3. Hatch Forward Support Arm
4. Camera Access Hatch
5. Sonne Amplifier Carriage (Fwd Bay)
6. Right Side Camera Window (Aft Bay)
7. Right Door and Step
8. Hatch Rear Support Arm
9. Location of Viewfinder
10. Crash Barrier
11. Left Door and Step
12. Viewfinder Compartment Access Cover (LH Only)
13. Window Washing Filler
14. Left Side Camera Window (Aft Bay)
15. Viewfinder Window
16. Bottom Camera Window (Aft Bay)
17. Sliding Nose Section Latch
18. Bottom Camera Window (Fwd Bay)
19. Scanner Window

COURTESY OF GRUMMAN AEROSPACE CORP.

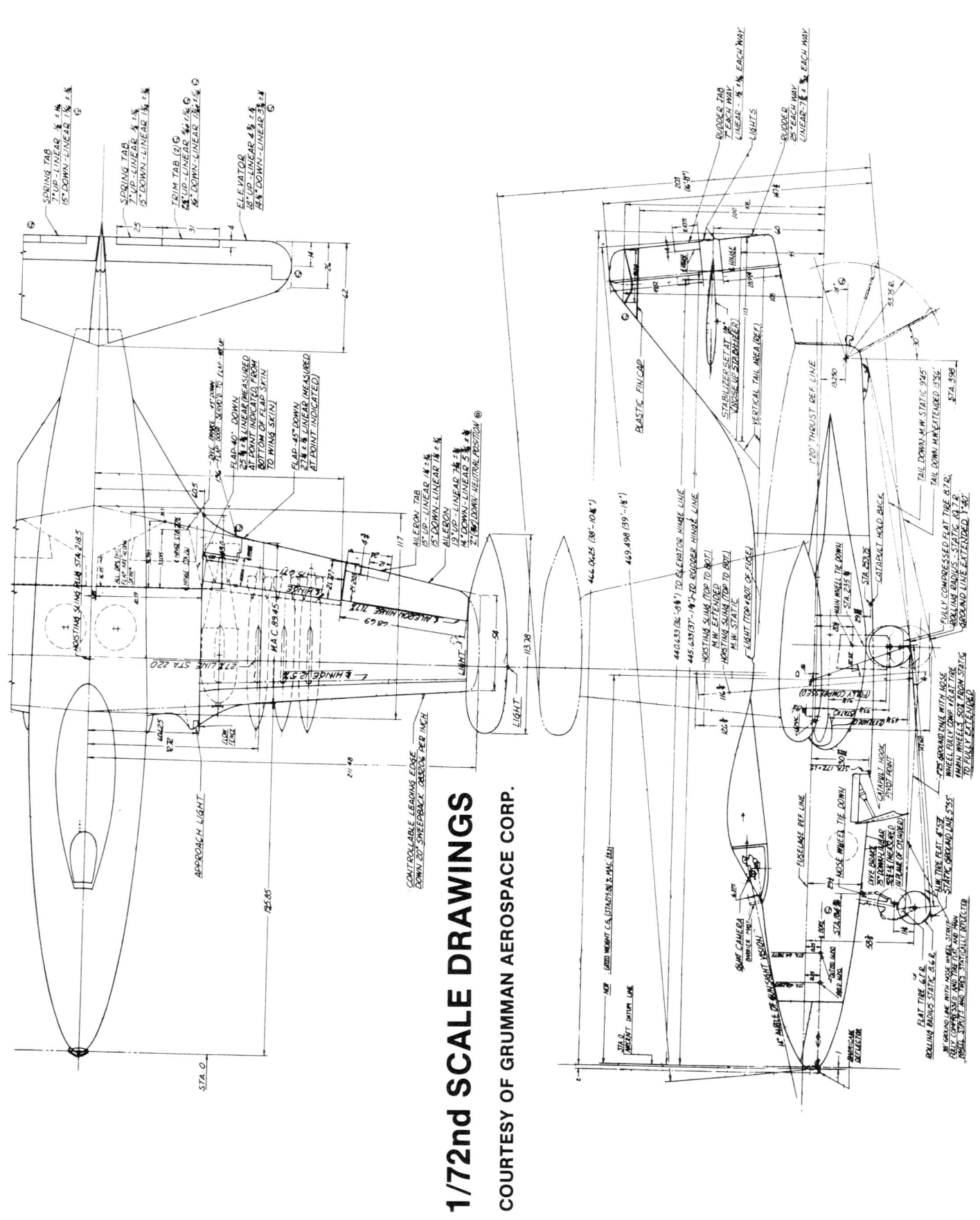

1/72nd SCALE DRAWINGS
COURTESY OF GRUMMAN AEROSPACE CORP.

F9F-4/5 DIMENSIONS

DIMENSION	ACTUAL	1/72nd SCALE	1/48th SCALE	1/32nd SCALE
Wingspan (Extended)	455.88 in.	6.33 in.	9.50 in.	14.25 in.
Wingspan (Folded)	295.0 in.	4.10 in.	6.15 in.	9.22 in.
Length (Normal)	466.06 in.	6.47 in.	9.71 in.	14.56 in.
Length (Nose Extended)	506.06 in.	7.03 in.	10.54 in.	15.81 in.
Tail Span	206.5 in.	2.87 in.	4.30 in.	6.45 in.
Height (To Top of Tail)	147.5 in.	2.05 in.	3.07 in.	4.61 in.
Height (To Top of Folded Wing)	203.0 in.	2.82 in.	4.23 in.	6.34 in.
Wheel Track	146.1 in.	2.03 in.	3.04 in.	4.57 in.
Wheel Tread	99.0 in.	1.38 in.	2.06 in.	3.09 in.

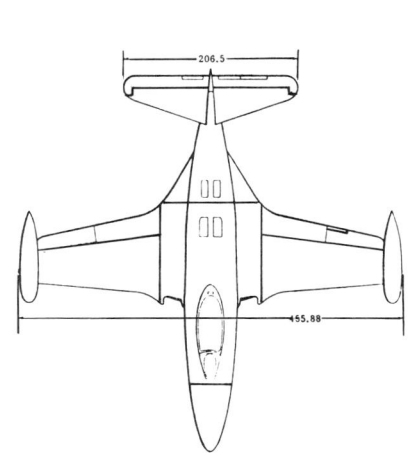
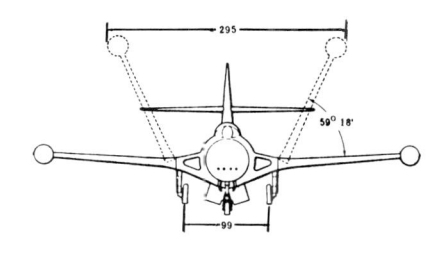
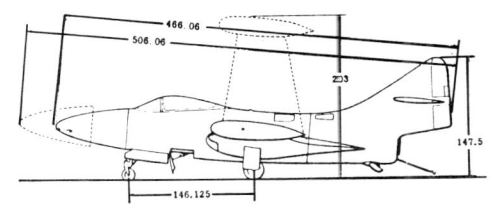

F9F-4/5 PANTHER

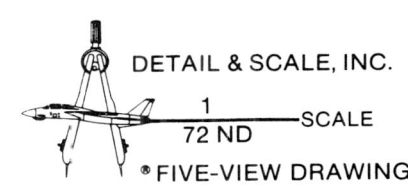

DETAIL & SCALE, INC.
1/72ND SCALE
FIVE-VIEW DRAWING

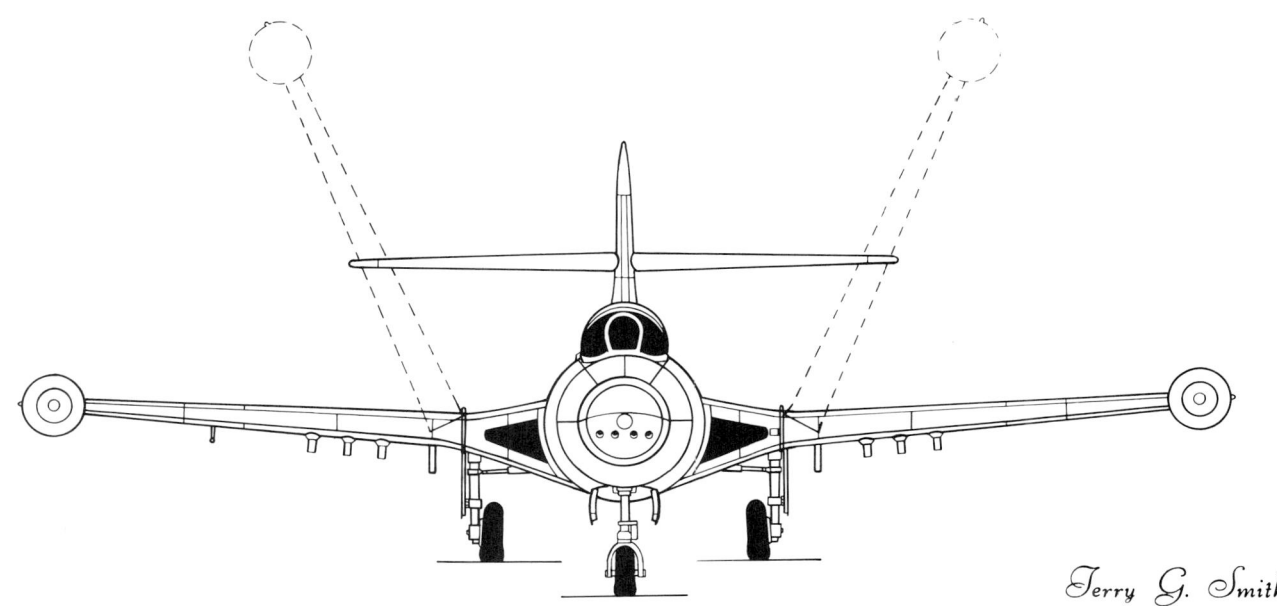

Jerry G. Smith

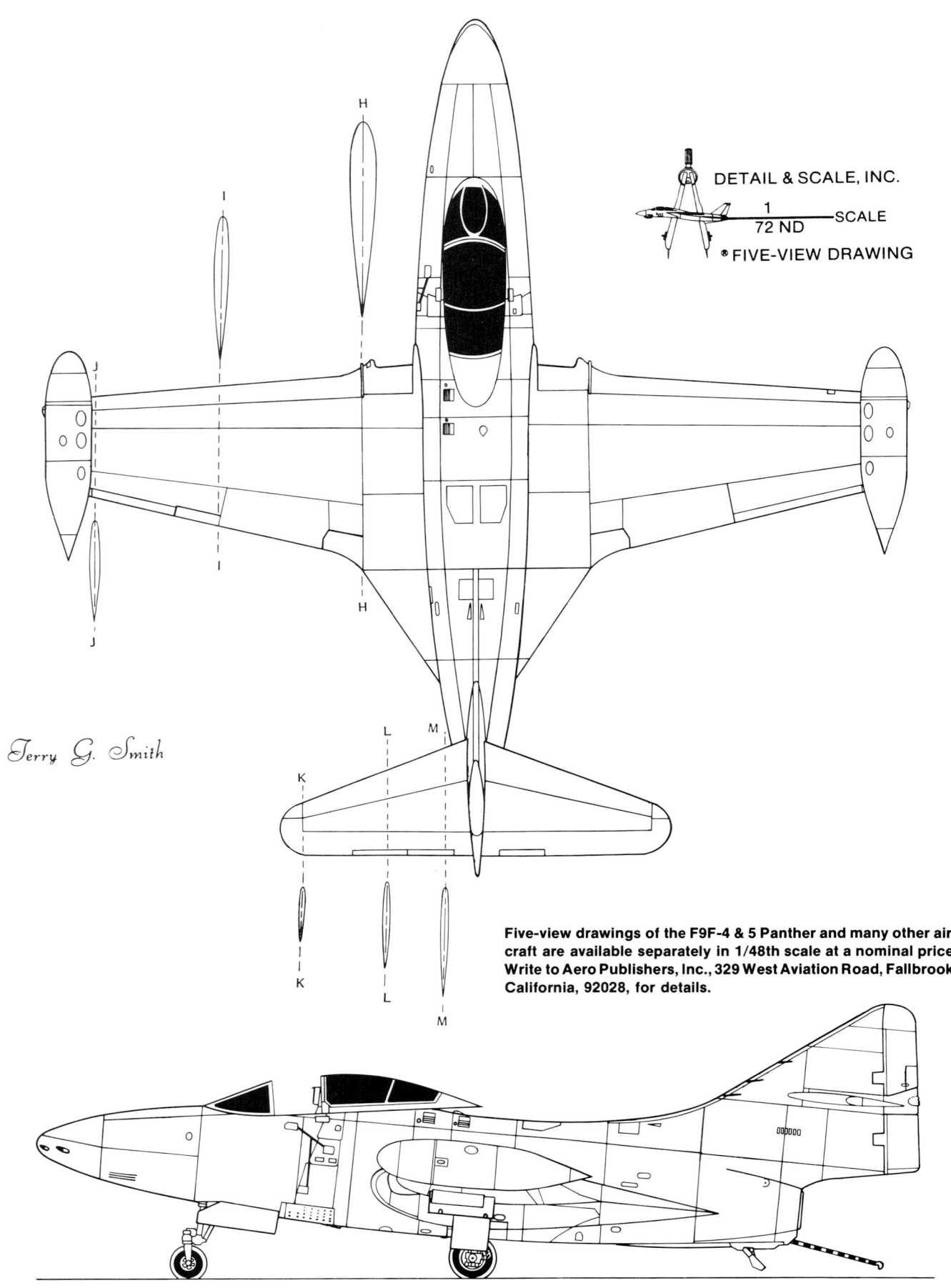

DETAIL & SCALE, INC.
1/72ND SCALE
® FIVE-VIEW DRAWING

Jerry G. Smith

Five-view drawings of the F9F-4 & 5 Panther and many other aircraft are available separately in 1/48th scale at a nominal price. Write to Aero Publishers, Inc., 329 West Aviation Road, Fallbrook, California, 92028, for details.

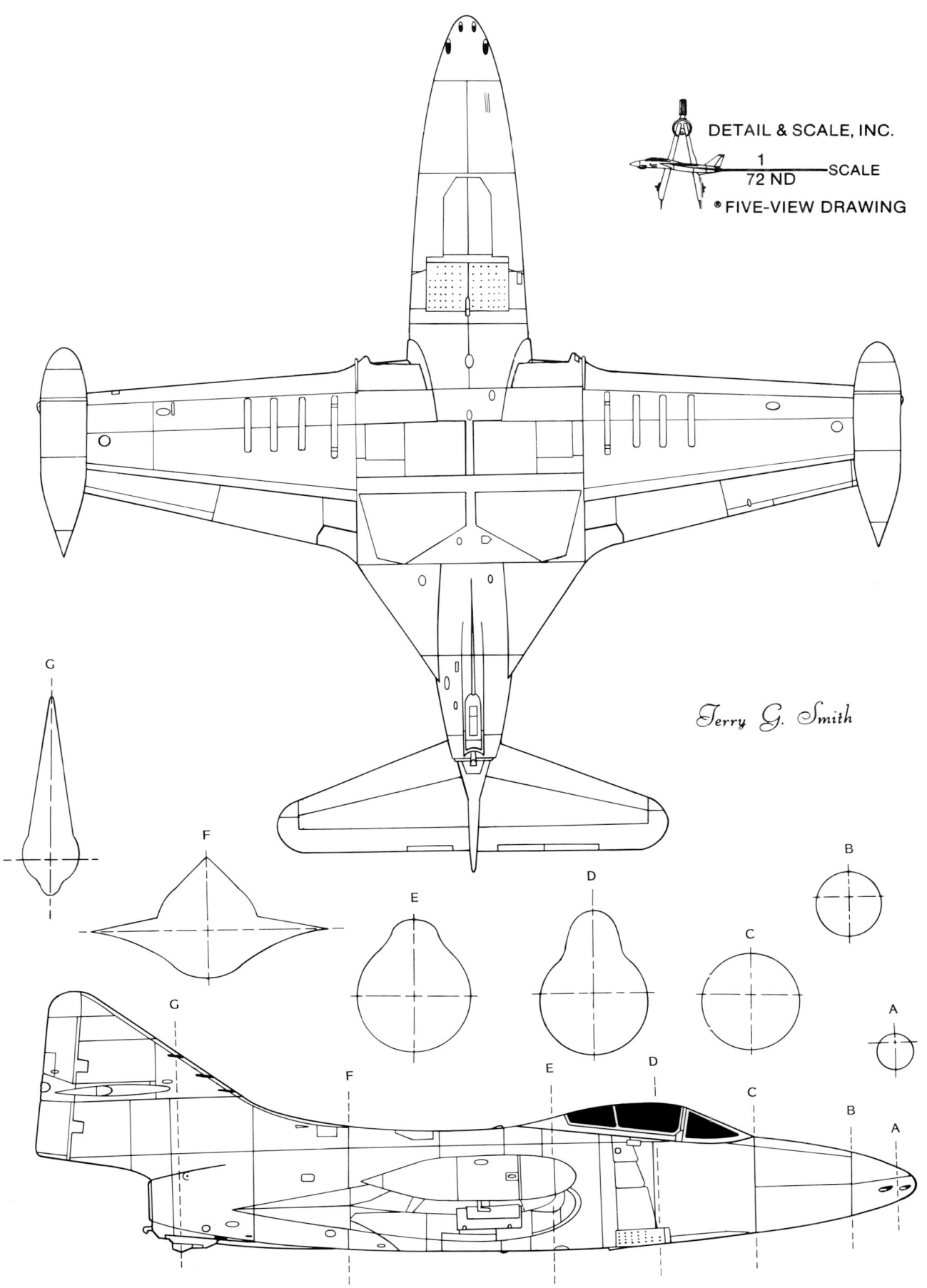

ARMAMENT & EXTERNAL STORES

An F9F-2 from VF-111 displays over 170 mission markings as it drops two bombs on communist positions in Korea. The aircraft is from the carrier USS Valley Forge, CV-45. (Grumman)

Panthers were tested with a number of loads. Here, sixteen 5 inch rockets are carried in pods. (National Archives)

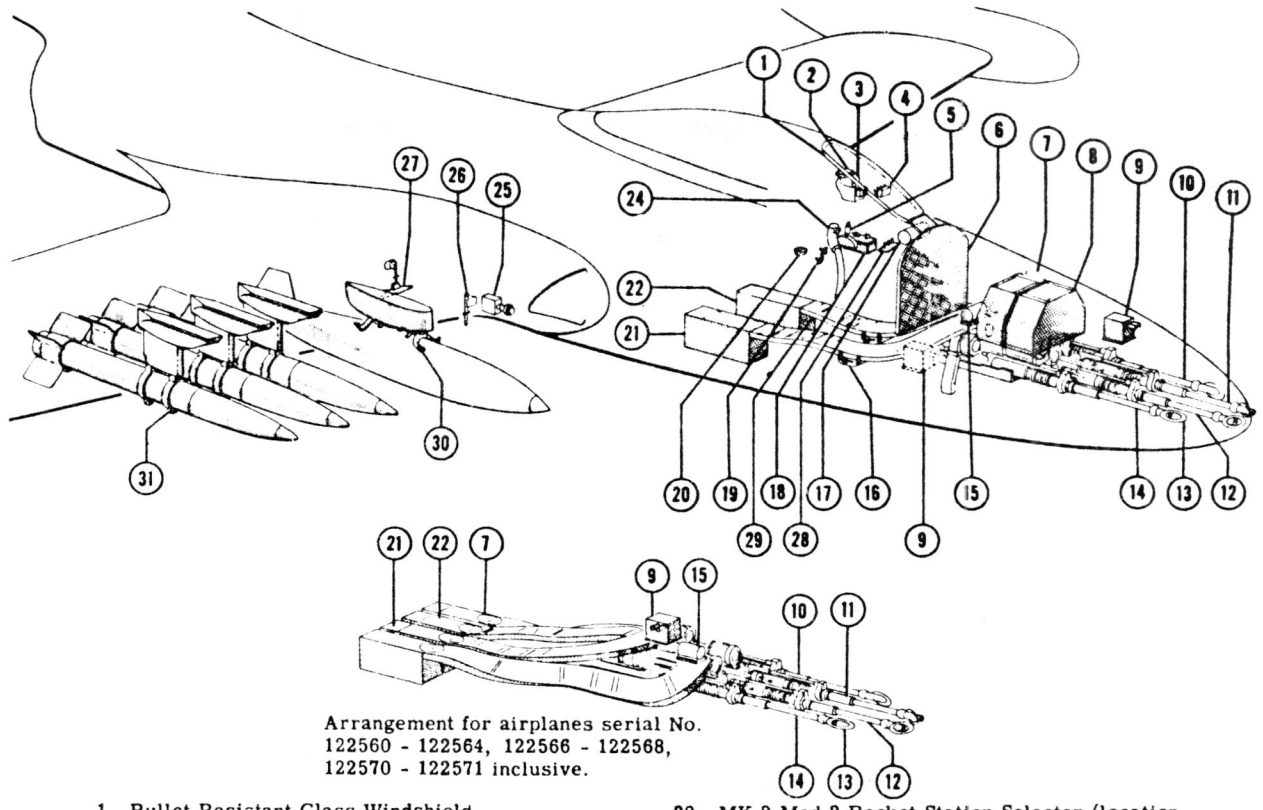

1. Bullet Resistant Glass Windshield
2. A.F.C.S. Camera
3. MK 8 Mod 0 Gunsight (A.F.C.S.)
4. Armament Switch Panel
5. Throttle Grip Ranging Control
6. Cockpit Forward Armor Plate
7. Gun No. 2 Ammunition Box
8. Gun No. 3 Ammunition Box
9. Relay Box (see Note)
10. Gun No. 1
11. Gun No. 2
12. Gun No. 3
13. Gun Blast Shields (4)
14. Gun No. 4
15. A.F.C.S. Voltage Regulator
16. Gun No. 1 Ammunition Feed Chute (with electric booster)
17. Gun Sight Controller
18. A.F.C.S. Electrical Control Box (on LH console)
19. A.F.C.S. Rocket Control Switches, Airplane ser No. 122560 - 123713 inclusive, if installed. (Guns - 5" HVAR and DIVE ANGLE - 35° AND OVER, 35° AND UNDER)
20. MK 2 Mod 2 Rocket Station Selector (location shown is for airplane ser No. 122560 - 123713 inclusive. If installed on airplane ser No. 125083 and subs, the selector is forward on the console adjacent to item 28.)
21. Gun No. 1 Ammunition Box
22. Gun No. 4 Ammunition Box
23. DELETED
24. Control Stick Grip with Gun and Rocket - Bomb Trigger Switches
25. Gun Camera
26. Forward Boresighting Rod
27. Rear Boresighting Rod
28. Rockets and Bombs Switch Panel, Airplane ser No. 125083 and subsequent (BOMB EMERGENCY RELEASE, GUNS - 5" HVAR, DIVE ANGLE - 35° AND OVER, 35° AND UNDER, RH MK 51 - SAFE LH - MK 51 - SAFE.)
29. Gun No. 4 Ammunition Feed Chute (with electric booster)
30. MK 51 Bomb Rack (L/R)
31. MK 9 Mod 2 Rocket Launchers (3L/3R) shown or MK 55 Mod 0 Bomb Racks (3L/3R)

ROCKET FIRING SEQUENCE

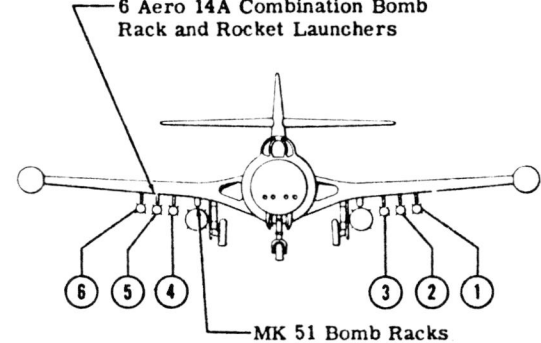

MK 2 Station Selector Setting	Single Release From Sta No.	Pair Release From Sta No's.
1	1	
2	5	
3	3	
4	6	6 and 1
5	2	5 and 2
6	4	All Remain

20 MM CANNON

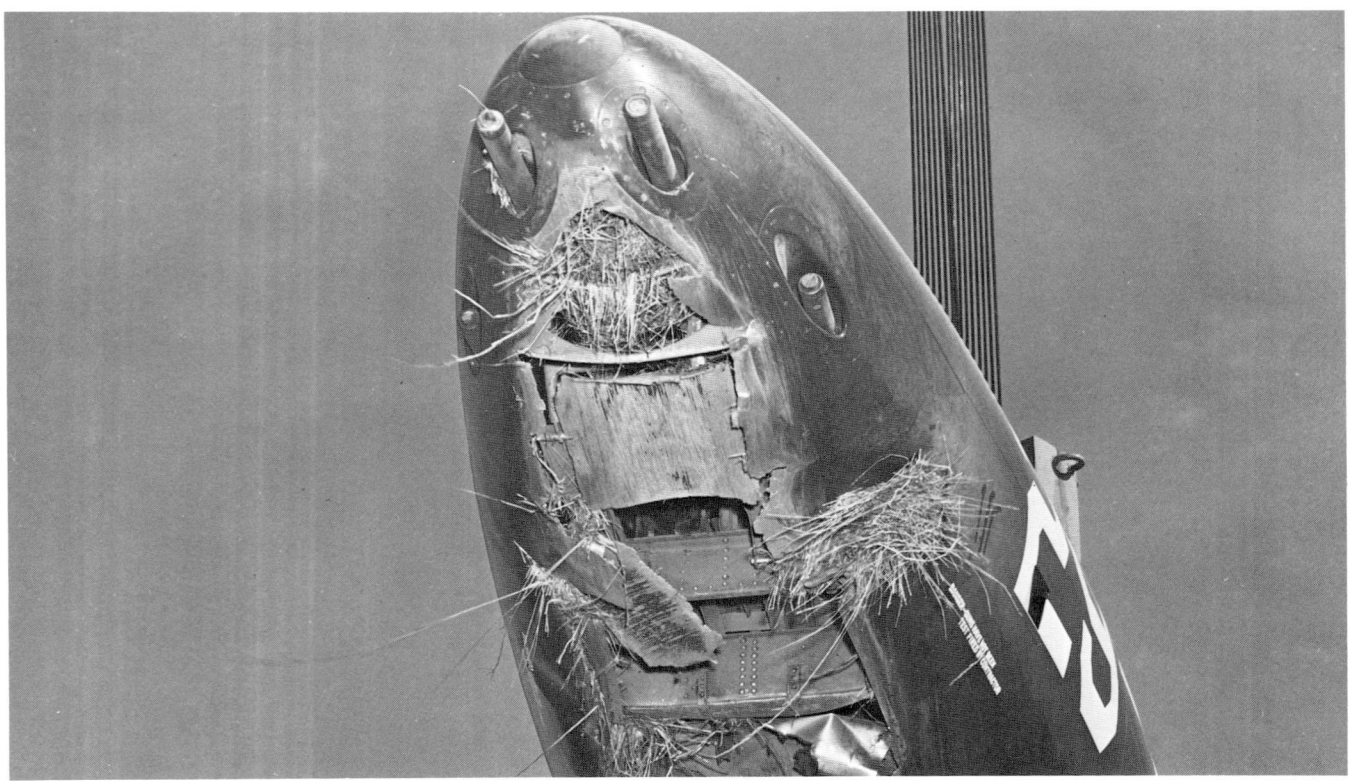
After literally "biting the dirt," this Panther's nose is all chewed up, but the photo reveals to good effect the locations of the guns and how far the barrels protruded from the gun ports. (Grumman)

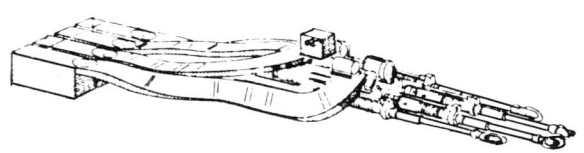

Arrangement for airplanes serial No.
122560 - 122564, 122566 - 122568,
122570 - 122571 inclusive.

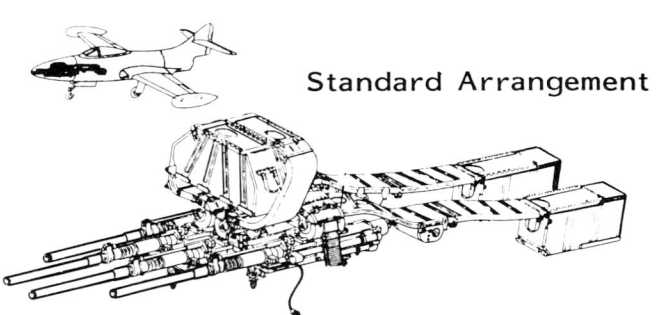

Standard Arrangement

There were two different arrangements for the ammunition boxes on Panthers. BuNos for the arrangement on the left are given. All others had the arrangement shown at right. (Drawings courtesy of Grumman)

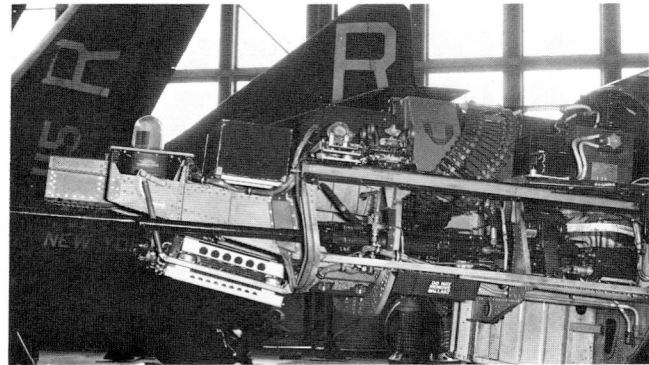

These two photos show right and left side views of the gun installation arrangement as found on most Panthers. (Grumman)

PYLONS & FUEL TANKS

Although rarely done, the Panther could carry external fuel tanks as seen here on this F9F-5P. (Grumman)

Here the larger MK 51 pylons are shown under the wing of an F9F-5. The wing tip fuel tank details are also clearly visible. Note the light and the filler cap just above it. Also visible is one of the vents for jettisoning the fuel at the aft end of the tank. (Grumman)

BOMBS

This F9F-2 is shown about to be launched from a carrier for a strike over Korea. Six 250 pound bombs are carried on the Aero 14A pylons which also are used for rockets. *(National Archives)*

Two flying shots show bombs being carried under the wings of Panthers. At left, four 250 pound bombs are carried on the smaller Aero 14A racks, while in the right photo, heavier bombs are attached to the larger MK 51 pylons on a test flight. *(Left Grumman; right, Williams via Lloyd)*

Here crewmen labor to load bombs on an F9F-5 while the wings are folded. *(National Archives)*

2.75 INCH ROCKETS

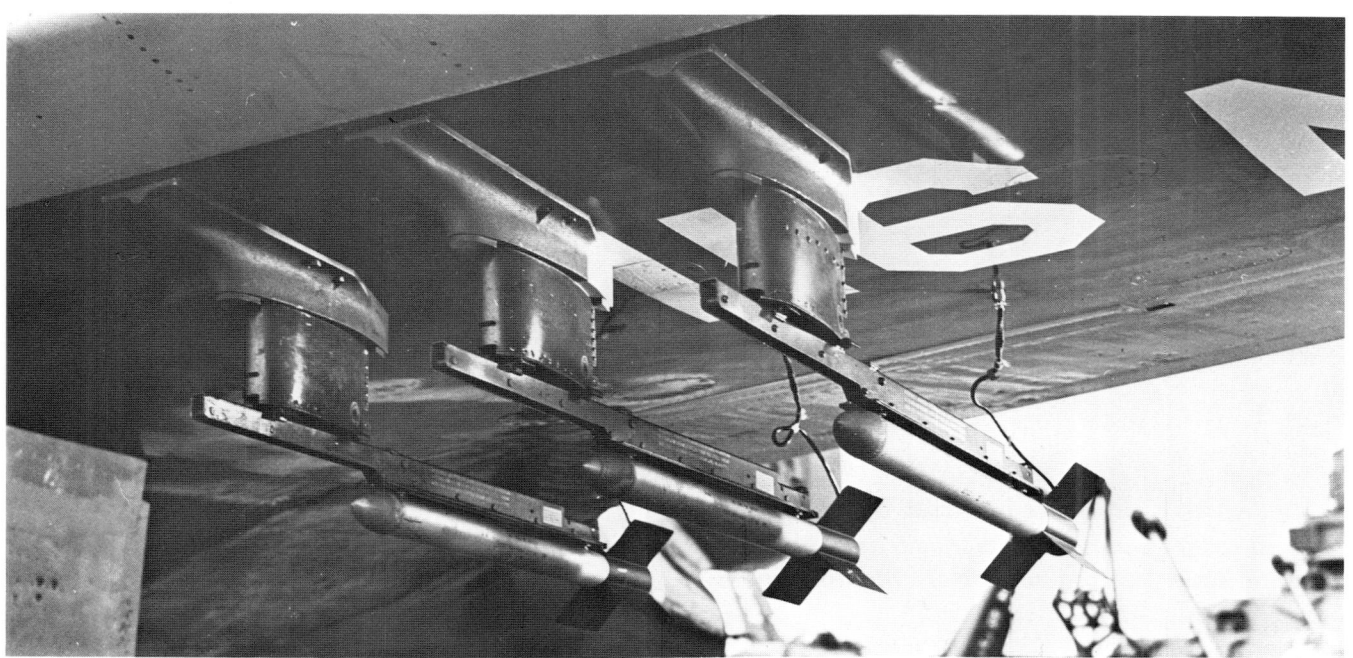

Although the rockets usually carried by the Panther were of the 5 inch HVAR variety, these smaller rockets were also used.

Above: Rockets seen from the front. Note the special launch rail attached to the Aero 14A rack.
(Grumman)

Right: Rockets seen from behind. Note the connected wires used for firing the rocket motors.
(Grumman)

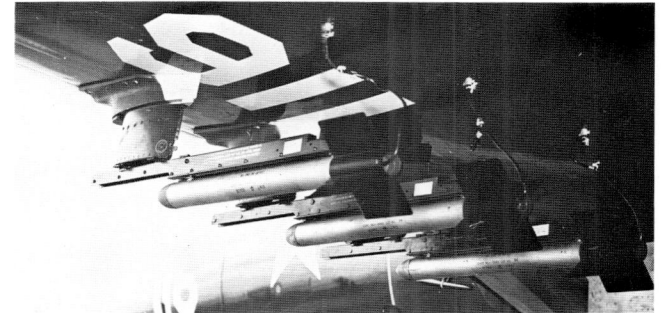

Rockets as seen on a folded wing of a Panther with wires disconnected. *(Grumman)*

5 INCH ROCKETS

Standard rocket armament included 5 inch HVAR rockets as shown here. Rockets had an olive drab warhead and a dull silver colored body. Note the firing wires. (Grumman)

At left is a photo of 5 inch rockets under the right wing of a Panther. At right crewmen load rockets on a VF-721 Panther in preparation for a strike over Korea. (National Archives)

These two photos show a test installation used for carrying sixteen HVAR rockets on a Panther. Note that MK 51 pylons are used. Covers were carried over the ends of the rocket launchers as shown at right, and were destroyed as the rockets were fired. (National Archives)

NAVY CARRIER-BASED PANTHER SQUADRONS USED IN THE KOREAN WAR

Unit	Type Used	Carrier	Tail Letter	Nose Number *	Dates
VF-23	F9F-2	CV-37, USS Princeton	M	200	6/1951 - 8/1951
VF-23	F9F-2	CV-9, USS Essex	M	200	7/1952 - 1/1953
VF-24	F9F-2	CV-37, USS Princeton	K	400	12/1950 - 5/1951
VF-24	F9F-2	CV-21, USS Boxer	M	400	3/1952 - 9/1952
VF-31	F9F-2	CV-32, USS Leyte	K	100	10/1950 - 1/1951
VF-34	F9F-2	CV-32, USS Leyte	K	200	10/1950 - 1/1951
VF-51	F9F-2	CV-45, USS Valley Forge	S	100	6/1950 - 11/1950
VF-51	F9F-2	CV-9, USS Essex	S	100	8/1951 - 3/1952
VF-51	F9F-5	CVA-45, USS Valley Forge	S	100	12/1952 - 6/1953
VF-52	F9F-2	CV-45, USS Valley Forge	S	200	6/1950 - 11/1950
VF-52	F9F-2	CV-45, USS Valley Forge	S	200	12/1951 - 6/1952
VF-52	F9F-5	CVA-21, USS Boxer	S	100	5/1953 - 7/1953
VF-53	F9F-5	CVA-45, USS Valley Forge	S	300	12/1952 - 6/1953
VF-71	F9F-2	CV-31, USS Bon Homme Richard	L	100	unknown
VF-72	F9F-2	CV-31, USS Bon Homme Richard	L	200	unknown
VF-91	F9F-2	CVA-47, USS Philippine Sea	N	100	1/1953 - 7/1953
VF-93	F9F-2	CVA-47, USS Philippine Sea	N	300	1/1953 - 7/1953
VF-111	F9F-2	CV-47, USS Philippine Sea	V	100	8/1950 - 3/1951
VF-111	F9F-2	CV-45, USS Valley Forge	S	100	12/1951 - 6/1952
VF-111	F9F-5	CVA-21, USS Boxer	V	100	5/1953 - 7/1953
VF-112	F9F-2	CV-47, USS Philippine Sea	V	200	8/1950 - 3/1951
VF-112	F9F-2	Cv-47, USS Philippine Sea	V	200	1/1952 - 7/1952
VF-113	F9F-2	CV-47, USS Philippine Sea	V	300	1/1952 - 7/1952
VF-151	F9F-5	CVA-21, USS Boxer	H	300	5/1953 - 7/1953
VF-153	F9F-5	CVA-37, USS Princeton	H	300	3/1953 - 7/1953
VF-154	F9F-5	CVA-37, USS Princeton	H	400	3/1953 - 7/1953
VF-191	F9F-2	CV-37, USS Princeton	B	100	12/1950 - 5/1951
VF-191	F9F-2	CV-37, USS Princeton	B	100	4/1952 - 10/1952
VF-721	F9F-2	CV-21, USS Boxer	A	100	3/1951 - 10/1951
VF-721	F9F-2	CV-33, USS Kearsarge	A	100	9/1952 - 2/1953
VF-781	F9F-2	CV-31, USS Bon Homme Richard	D	100	5/1951 - 11/1951
VF-781	F9F-5	CVA-34, USS Oriskany	D	100	10/1952 - 5/1953
VF-783	F9F-5	CVA-34, USS Oriskany	D	200	10/1952 - 5/1953
VF-821	F9F-2	CV-9, USS Essex	A	300	7/1952 - 1/1953
VF-831	F9F-2	CV-36, USS Antietam	H	300	10/1951 - 3/1952
VF-837	F9F-2	CV-36, USS Antietam	H	400	10/1951 - 3/1952

NOTES:

In addition to the units listed above, detachments from VC-61 operated F9F-2P's and F9F-5P's (as well as a few F2H-2P Banshees) on most carriers listed above. These aircraft carried the tail code "PP."

All Essex class carriers in Korea except for CVA-39, USS Lake Champlain, carried at least one fighter squadron equipped with Panthers. The Lake Champlain had two squadrons of F2H-2 Banshees (VF-22 and VF-62), and was on station off Korea from June 10, 1953 to July 27, 1953.

*Nose numbers were three digit numbers painted on each side of the nose. The numbers on the chart above represent the first number in the sequence for each squadron. For example, "200" means that all aircraft in the squadron have a number beginning with 2, and the sequence starts with 200, 201, 202, etc.

F9F-3 Aircraft were often mixed in with units operating F9F-2's.

NAVY PANTHERS

Two VF-151 Panthers are shown returning to the USS Wasp CV-18. Note the recovery helicopter off the starboard side of the ship. *(Grumman)*

This F9F-2 from VF-52 has the wing fence retrofitted just outboard of the intake. This was a standard feature on the later F9F-5. *(U.S. Navy)*

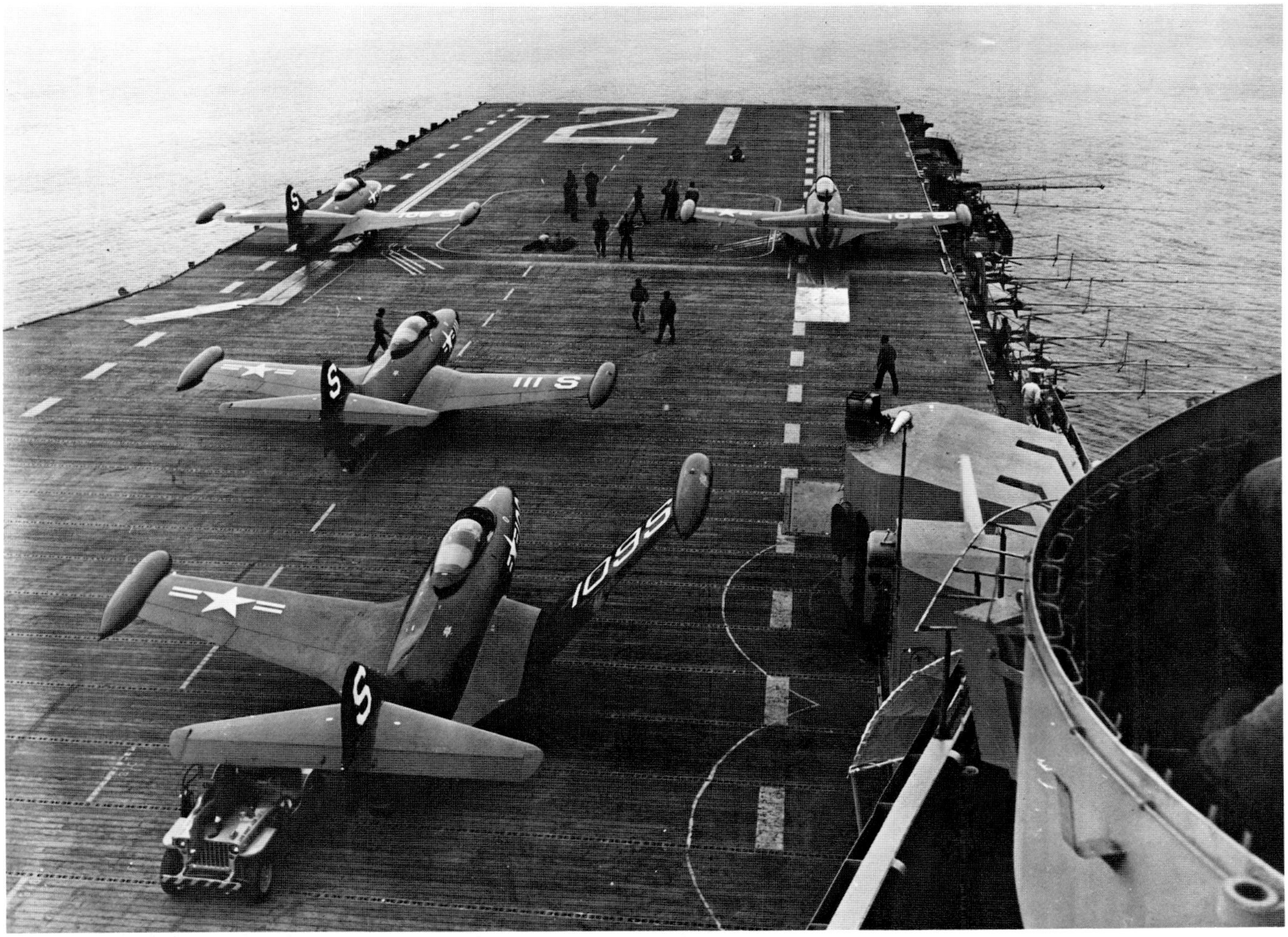

Panthers preparing to launch from the USS Boxer, CV-21. (Grumman)

VF-721 Panther over Korea. (Grumman)

As one F9F is freed from the arresting gear, another receives a wave-off since the deck is not ready. Yet another, which shows up as a speck above the left wing tip of the landed aircraft, turns onto final for its landing. (U.S. Navy)

MARINE PANTHERS

Crewmen watch as three bomb-laden Panthers are prepared for take-off in Korea. Three other Panthers, already on their way to targets appear as small blurry specks overhead. (USMC Photo)

Marine Panthers receive servicing between strikes in Korea. (USMC Photo)

Armed with rockets, this F9F-2 is fueled prior to a strike in Korea. (USMC Photo)

This Marine Panther skips over the barrier and collapses its nose gear on landing. The photo shows the lowered leading edge flaps to good effect. (Grumman)

VMF-311 F9F-2Bs are shown receiving fuel in Korea. Korean air strips were crude, and as anyone who has spent a year in Korea knows, climatic conditions can range from extreme heat and humidity in the summer to bone chilling cold in the winter. This was a real test for aircraft and men alike. Note the lights on the trailing edge of the vertical tail. (USMC Photo)

Fueling and arming operations take place at the same time as seen in these two photos. At left, the guns are being loaded with ammunition, fuel is going into the fuselage tanks, and rockets are being loaded under the wing. At right, crewmen load a rocket while another fuels the fuselage tanks. Needless to say, there was no smoking when these operations were in progress. (USMC Photos)

BLUE ANGELS

The Blue Angels are shown here in their first jets. These first Panthers used by the Blue Angels did not have tip tanks. (US Navy)

A line-up of Blue Angel's F9F-2s are seen here with wings folded. (Grumman)

F9F-5s were also flown by the Blue Angels. Here, number 2, left, and the number 3, right, pose for the camera in their spotless blue and gold finish. (Grumman)

The Blue Angels fly in formation in tall-tailed F9F-5s. It is unusual to see number 2 on the right wing and number 3 on the left wing. (Grumman)

This photo of the Blue Angels was taken high over NAS Jacksonville on January 13, 1953. (Grumman)

This impressive shot, taken straight down on the diamond formation, shows the lack of wing markings. Because of their clear lines, Panthers were beautiful aircraft for formation flying. (Grumman)

This photo shows the formation take-off used by the Blue Angels. (Williams via Lloyd)

MODELER'S SECTION

PRODUCT REVIEW POLICY. In each of our publications we will try to review kits and decals that are available to the scale modeler. We hope to be able to review every currently available kit that is useable by the scale modeler. Kits produced in the past that are no longer generally available, and those more intended to be toys than accurate scale models will not usually be covered. Additionally, we do not intend to give a complete step-by-step correction-by-correction account of how to build each kit. Instead we intend to give a brief description of what is available to the modeler, and point out some of the good and not-so-good points of each kit or product. In this way we hope to give an overall picture of what the modeler has readily available for his use in building the particular aircraft involved.

KIT REVIEWS

1/72nd SCALE KITS

Airmodel F9F-2 Kit

This vacu-formed model is covered in the 1/72nd scale section, but its measurements just don't check out. The wingspan in 1/72nd scale should be 6.33 inches, but the span on the model falls short of six inches even. The length is too long, being over 6.5 inches when it should be only 6.32 inches. Likewise, the proportions of the model look all wrong, being too fat looking. The sleek look of the Panther just is not there. Even the fuel tanks are too thick and not long enough.

Surface scribing is recessed, and rather oversized and crude. It is not very accurate. For example, the blow-in doors are too long and narrow. As with most vacu-formed kits, detail parts for the landing gear, cockpit, and any external stores must come from the parts box or be built from scratch.

The one point in this kit's favor is that it is a good vacu-formed kit for beginners. Assembly is straight forward, and it gives the modeler a chance to learn the basics of building a vacu-formed model. By using the scale drawings in this book, and parts from a Minicraft T-33 and the spares box, and with a lot of patience, the inexperienced modeler can build an attractive, if not altogether accurate, model of the Panther.

Matchbox F9F-4, Kit Number PK-124

The most recently released of all the injected molded kits of the Panther is this offering from Matchbox. It represents an F9F-4, and can also be used to build an F9F-5, since the two were externally identical. Parts come on three colored trees, one dark blue, one light blue, and one black. The clear canopy is provided separately. It has fine raised scribing for most panels, but control surfaces, main gear doors, leading edge flaps, trim tabs, and blow-in doors are all represented by recessed scribing which is a bit on the heavy side. Dimensions and shapes seem to be accurate, but several of the small parts are not well detailed. The worst of these is the seat and the wheels.

The kit provides an option for building the model with the wings folded. While this is a nice idea, Matchbox placed the wing fence on the folding part of the wing when it should be on the part that does not fold. This can be seen clearly in the photo on the rear cover of this book. Additionally, the fence is too thick and incorrectly shaped. It should be replaced with one made from thin plastic card.

The cockpit consists of a tub with consoles, floor, and aft bulkhead. A nice control column is provided, but, as mentioned before, the seat is very bad. Most modelers will probably want to rework it and add some detail if the canopy is to be displayed in the open position. Since the canopy is molded in one piece, it will have to be cut if it is to be opened, but this is a simple task. The instrument panel was made to fit the model, and is not the same shape as the real thing. It will take some reworking and detailing to look right.

Prior to the release of the Minicraft and Matchbox injection molded kits, this vacu-formed offering by Airmodel was the only kit of the Panther in 1/72nd scale.

The Matchbox Panther is the only 1/72nd scale kit that represents an F9F-5 version.

The simple solution is to use an instrument panel decal from the Minicraft kit or a Microscale sheet, and then use the canopy in the closed position. This is not real effective, but it does "make do" without a lot of work if a basic model is all that is required. A pilot figure can be used to hide the lack of seat detail, but a better one than is supplied in this kit should be found.

Assembly is straight forward except that this is the only kit of the Panther that has the fuselage halves split top and bottom rather than in two side pieces. The vertical tail is two separate pieces split left and right. Eight pylons are provided, as are four 1,000 pound bombs and six 5 inch rockets. A full length tail hook is included, and can be displayed in the extended position. Wheel wells and the speed brake well have ample depth, but no detailing.

With care and some reworking, this kit can be built into a nice model of a "second generation" Panther. It is considerably better than many of the Matchbox kits that we have seen. With some work and homemade conversion parts, it can be built into an early F9F-6 or F9F-7 Cougar. With the proper amount of reworking and correcting, we recommend this kit.

Minicraft 1/72nd scale F9F-2. This is the best Panther kit available in any scale.

Minicraft/Hasegawa F9F-2, Kit Number 1138

This is easily the best Panther kit on the market. It is effectively designed, and even built straight from the box, it makes for a very nice model. The two-piece canopy fits open or closed over a cockpit that features a floor/console combination, nice seat, control column, and instrument panel. Decals are provided for the instrument panel and consoles, and will be sufficient for many modelers in this scale. However, one error should be noted. The consoles are flat rather than being stepped as they were in the F9F-2 and -3.

Dimensions, proportions, and shape are all correct except for the nose. The nose centerline is on the aircraft centerline, and it should be below it. Correcting this would be rather difficult since it is the shape of the nose that is wrong and not the angle at which it is molded on the fuselage. Also in the nose, the gun barrels are too long, but this is easily corrected.

All details are nicely done except that the spokes in the main wheels are not correct. The intakes have interiors (parts 8 and 9) and a tail pipe is also provided. This eliminates the hollow look that is a problem with the older kits. Six 5 inch rockets are provided, as are their launch racks. The racks, however, are too long in chord and should be shortened a bit.

Except for the nose being the wrong shape, all errors in this kit are quite small and easily corrected. We recommend this model as the best available of the Panther.

Folding the wings on a Minicraft Panther is simple, and takes little time. Even a relatively inexperienced modeler can perform the required surgery.

1/48th SCALE KITS

Aurora F9F-3 Kit

This is the oldest Panther kit on the market, and it shows its age. It is hollow, meaning that you can look in the intakes and see out the tail. Decal locations are scribed in the plastic, and there is no cockpit. A pilot's head is molded into the fuselage halves. There are no wheel wells. In the case of the main gear, the strut, door, and wheel are all molded as one piece which locates in a hole under the wing. For the nose gear, the strut and wheel are split vertically, and are molded to the appropriate nose gear door. Representing the XF9F-3, the model has no guns or tail bumper skid. It does have a long boom for the nose and two racks of four 5 inch rockets. The BuNo., scribed into the tail, is 123558, and is for an F9F-2.

It must be kept in mind that this kit comes from the early fifties, and modeling was far less sophisticated then. For a thirty year old kit, it is not all that bad, and forms the basis for a complete rework into a detailed model. However its value now lies mostly with collectors.

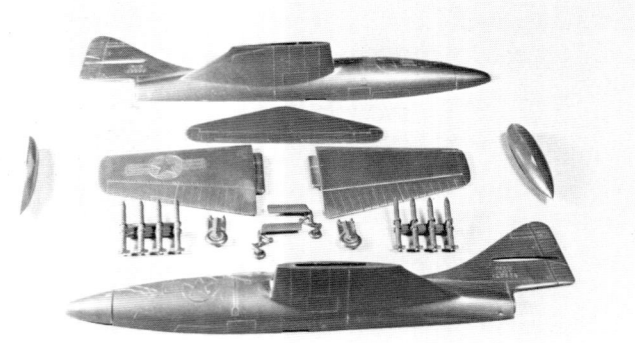

The first plastic Panther was the 1/48th scale kit from Aurora. It was based on the XF9F-3, and is very crude by today's standards. However, it is more accurate in outline than the AMT kit issued some twenty years later.

Hawk F9F-3, Kit Number 400

This kit is almost as old as the Aurora kit, and is of practically the same design. This time there is a hole in the cockpit area where a crosspiece forms the seat for a pilot figure. Although the kit provides a rather crude landing gear, it is not shown on the instruction sheet, and we built our model in the gear-up in-flight configuration.

With BuNo. 122564 on the tail, the model represents the third F9F-3, but has no guns or bumper skid. The boom is provided for the nose as it was in the Aurora kit. For our sample model, we reworked the nose, added guns, and detailed the cockpit before putting it on the kit-provided display stand. We also filled in the inner walls of the intakes, and added a tail pipe and bumper skid. Four bombs come in the kit that are to be attached to two small stubs under the wings. Rockets are also provided, but there are no provisions for mounting them. But it would be a simple matter to make racks from plastic stock to which stores can be added.

It would be nice to see Testors rework this kit for a re-release as they have done with other Hawk kits. The potential is there, but much work would have to be done. However it would easily be better than the AMT kit which is covered next.

The old Hawk F9F is basically the same as the Aurora kit in 1/48th scale. It really shows its age, and is hard to find.

AMT F9F-2 Kit

This is one of the worst post-1970 kits that we have seen. Its shape is all wrong, and the fit of the parts is terrible. It seems that the parts were designed to fit together in the worst possible places. For example, the top and bottom of the wings join at the leading edges, which is fine, and in the middle of the flaps and ailerons on the underside. This forms a bad joint in the worst possible place for filling and sanding, and causes a mold mark on the upper surfaces opposite the seam. The natural place to join the wings would be at the trailing edge or the natural line between the wing and the flap and aileron on the underside. The same problem exists with the horizontal stabilizers, which have the added problem of joining the vertical tail about one quarter the way out on their span. Again, this is an unnatural place for a joint, and makes sanding and filling most difficult. The natural thing to do would be to have the horizontal stabilizer be all one piece and fit through a slot in the vertical tail, or have left and right horizontal stabilizers each glued to the proper side of the vertical tail. Assembled the way it comes in the kit, there is almost no way to get a smooth skin on the horizontal stabilizers.

The fuselage is way too fat, and guns protrude too far from the nose. It really is impossible to get the fuselage to look like the sleek shape of a Panther. Small parts, such as landing gear, speed brakes, intakes, and tail pipe are very crude. If the modeler really wants to build a quarter scale Panther, it would be better to start with one of the older kits covered above.

1/32nd SCALE KIT

Combat Models F9F-5, Kit Number 32-33

This vacu-formed kit from Combat Models provides the basics for building a 1/32nd scale Panther. Dimensions and shape are generally good, as is the molding. The one exception is the horizontal stabilizer which will require some reworking. Scribing is a bit heavy, and is inaccurate in some places.

For example, the outer main gear doors are not scribed in, and the inner flaps are scribed in completely wrong. See the drawings in this book for the correct shape and proportions.

A cockpit "tub," seat, and wheels are all provided, but it would be better to replace them with parts from other kits. Pylons and ordnance would be easy to add also. Being an F9F-5, the kit has the modified intakes, but no wing fences. These can be made from plastic card. We would suggest that anyone desiring to build this kit first get a copy of our five-view drawing set on the F9F-4/5 Panther, DS-48-10. Ordering information can be obtained by writing Aero Publishers, Inc., 329 West Aviation Road, Fallbrook, California 92028. These large scale drawings will provide a good source of reference to work from during construction, and are more detailed than those provided in the kit.

With work required by all vacu-formed models, this can be built into a nice model of the Panther.

In 1/32nd scale, Combat Models offers this vacu-formed model of the Panther. It is one of the simpler 1/32nd scale vacu-formed kits available.
(Combat Models)

DECAL SUMMARY

Note: It is impossible to completely review decals unless the reviewer has actually used the decals on a model to see how they fit. Additionally, markings on a given aircraft can be changed from time to time, so it is possible that the decals may be accurate for one point in time and not another. Therefore, this section is more of a listing of decals available than a review. Review comments are made only in regard to fit when we have actually used the decals or as to accuracy when the evidence clearly indicated an error.

1/72nd SCALE KITS

Matchbox F9F-4, Kit Number PK-124: Contains markings for two Panthers.
- F9F-4, 125939, VMF-314, in the overall blue scheme. The nose number is 8, and the tail code is LW.
- F9F-5, 126071, in the Blue Angels scheme for aircraft number 3.

Minicraft/Hasegawa F9F-2, Kit Number 1138: Contains markings for three aircraft.
- F9F-2, 123534, VF-123, in the overall blue scheme. The nose number is 307, and the tail code is D.
- F9F-2, 125091, VMF-115, in the overall blue scheme. The nose number is 17, and the tail code is AE.
- F9F-2, in the Blue Angels scheme for aircraft number 5.

1/48th SCALE KITS

Aurora F9F-3 Kit: Contains basic markings for an F9F-3 with an F9F-2 BuNo., 123558. The Panther logo is on the nose. This logo was used on the prototype Panthers.

Hawk F9F-3, Kit Number 400: Provides basic markings for the third F9F-3, 122564, and like the Aurora kit, has the Panther logo on the nose.

AMT F9F-2 Kit: Contains markings for an F9F-2, 123526, VMF-311, with a nose number of 3 and a tail code of WL.

1/72nd SCALE SHEETS

Microscale Sheet Number 72-206: Provides markings for four aircraft.
- F9F-2, with an erroneous BuNo., ATU-206, in the gull gray over white scheme.
- F9F-2, 123668, VF-721, in the overall blue scheme. The nose number is 124, and the tail code is A.
- F9F-2, 123534, VF-123, in the overall blue scheme. The tail code is D.
- F9F-3, VMF-311, in the overall blue scheme. The tail code is WL.

Notes: There are several bad errors in this sheet that should be noted.
- F9F-2 from ATU-206. The BuNo. for this aircraft given on the sheet is 127534 which is incorrect for any Panther. A photograph of this aircraft can be seen on page 43 of this book, and the first four digits are obviously 1236. They are in the large style, and not the small size numbers as provided by Microscale. The instruction sheet states that the rudder color is unknown, and it fails to point out that the elevators are also painted this same color. This lack of information and wrong BuNo. makes building an accurate model impossible. This aircraft has the antenna fairing added under the nose, and has the wing fences retrofitted. These parts are not in the Minicraft kit for which these decals are intended, yet there is no mention of these necessary changes made on the instruction sheet. The painting instructions fail to inform the modeler that the upper surfaces of the flaps and ailerons are painted white. There is an orange trim on the nose of this aircraft, but no decal nor painting instructions are provided for it. Intake warning and the warning on the tail section are not covered on the instructions. The latter is not provided on the decal sheet. In short, the decals provided and the instructions are completely inadequate to build this aircraft accurately.
- F9F-2, 123668. This aircraft was an F9F-2B, and was marked accordingly. The instruction sheet drawing shows the F9F-2B marking, but the callout and the decal show only F9F-2. The red nose flash does not fit the nose at all, and must be hand painted.
- F9F-2, 123534. There are no bad errors for this aircraft. The instructions do not clearly show where all of the decals go, and these are exactly the same markings as provided in the Minicraft kit. This makes one wonder why another scheme was not chosen in order to give the modeler a wider choice.
- F9F-3 from VMF-311. The instructions show this to be an F9F-3, but the call out and the decal read F9F-2, which is an error. It is an F9F-3. Microscale admits not knowing the BuNo. for this aircraft, which makes one wonder why this aircraft was chosen as a subject. They give 125092 as a fictitious number, and provide a "number jungle" to allow the modeler to make up his own number!

Microscale Sheet Number 72-212: Provides markings for four F9F-5s.
- F9F-5, 126078, VF-192, in the overall blue scheme. The nose number is 216, and the tail code is B.
- F9F-5, 125577, VMF-223, in the gull gray over white scheme. The nose number is 24, and the tail code is WP.
- F9F-5, 126960, VF-144, in the overall blue scheme. The nose number is 412, and the tail code is A.
- F9F-5, 126549, VF-114, CVG-11, CAG aircraft in the overall blue scheme. The nose number is 00, and the tail code is V.

Notes: This sheet provides conversion parts for the taller tail and the fairing under the nose. While this is a good idea, and we would like to see more of it, it falls far short in this case. The instructions make no mention of the fact that the fuselage has to be lengthened ahead of the wing roots, and no mention is made to, nor parts provided for, the wing fences. No mention is made as to the change required for the air intakes. The instructions state that the nose fairing belongs on 125577, and, "possibly one of the others." This makes the modeler wonder just which aircraft has it. To clear this up, we have photographs of all of these aircraft, and none of the others have the fairing. Comments on each of the aircraft are as follows.
- F9F-5, 126078. The instructions state that this aircraft was Lt. Brubaker's (William Holden's) in the movie,

"Bridges at Tokorie." (SIC). The movie was "Bridges at Toko-Ri," and this was not Brubaker's aircraft. At the beginning of the movie, Brubaker ditched 211, then flew 209, BuNo. 125598, for the rest of the movie. At no time did he fly 216. The instructions further state that "Lt Brubaker" was stenciled on the side near the cockpit. What was actually stenciled was, "LT. H. BRUBAKER," and it was in yellow stencilling on both sides of the cockpit. In the painting instructions Microscale says that the wing roots were golden yellow. They were not. Instead, they were the same aluminum color as the leading edges of the wing.

- F9F-5, 126920. The instructions for painting this aircraft state that it was gloss white overall. It was light gull gray over white. The nose and tail decals are a very poor fit. See page 36 in this book for a photo of this aircraft.
- F9F-5, 126960. The markings for the fuel tanks on this aircraft are wrong in that they continue forward on the insides of the tanks. They should make an angle at the top of each tank, and then extend back to the leading edge of the wing. The flash under the nose number is too long. It should stop under the forward most point of the national insignia, and be located entirely on the sliding portion of the nose. The location of the national insignia relative to the nose number is incorrect. They should almost touch. Modelers should note that this aircraft did not have the aluminum colored leading edges to the wings.
- F9F-5, 126549. The decals for this aircraft have four multi-colored rings that fit on the nose. The design should be a spiral instead.

Microscale Sheet Number 72-302: Provides markings for four aircraft, one of which is F9F-5, 125082. The aircraft is in the overall blue scheme. The nose number is 00, and the tail code is M.

Notes: The instruction sheet recommends the Hasegawa (Minicraft) F9F-5 kit. However, that kit is for an F9F-2, not an F9F-5. Obviously the decals for the rudder were designed to fit the Hasegawa F9F-2 tail, which is different from the F9F-5 which this aircraft is. The decals could be used on a Matchbox kit, but the tail stripes would have to be corrected by hand to fit the taller tail.

Microscale Sheet Number 72-333: Provides markings for three aircraft, one of which is an F9F-2, 123484, from VF-72, CVG-7, in the overall blue scheme. The nose number is 206, and the tail code is L.

Notes: On one side of the instruction sheet, a drawing shows this aircraft in the overall blue scheme. On the opposite side, a drawing is shown for the data placement. In this drawing, a bare metal scheme is represented, and includes markings not used on blue aircraft. This leaves the modeler confused on how to mark the aircraft.

Microscale Sheet Number 72-343: This sheet provides data stencils for the Panther.

Notes: Stencils are provided for both the blue scheme and the bare metal scheme. Although not mentioned on the instruction sheet, the ones for the bare metal scheme can also be used for the gray over white scheme. The instructions are nicely done and are easy to read. This is an excellent sheet that will highlight any 1/72nd scale Panther model.

1/48th SCALE SHEET

Microscale Sheet Number 48-60: Provides markings for four F9F-2s.
- F9F-2, 125091, VMF-115, in the overall blue scheme. The nose number is 17, and the tail code is AE.
- F9F-2, 123592, VF-91, in the overall blue scheme. The nose number is 108, and the tail code is N.
- F9F-2, 123558, VMF-223, in the overall blue scheme. The nose number is 16, and the tail code is WP.
- F9F-2, 123534, VF-123, in the overall blue scheme. The nose number is 307, and the tail code is D.

Notes:
- F9F-2, 125091. Microscale erroneously used the number 125081 on the decal sheet. The fact that the trailing tips of the fuel tanks are aluminum is not noted.
- F9F-2, 123592. Fit of the nose decal is poor. The instructions show a marking under the left wing, but it is not clear what it is and no decals are provided for it as far as we can tell.
- F9F-2, 123558. The word NAVY is missing between the F9F-2 and the BuNo. on the tail. Again, a marking is partly visible under the left wing on the instruction sheet, but it is unclear what it is. Another marking is partly visible on the left gear door. No decals are provided to go under the wing.
- F9F-2, 123534. Markings under the left wing are not clearly visible. Four full views are necessary to provide full coverage of where all the decals go.

Details make the difference.

Now ready for landing, the two newest titles in Kalmbach's Detail & Scale series.

The F-89 Scorpion (Detail & Scale series vol. 41)

Conduct a nose-to-tail inspection of the 1950s-era nuclear-armed jet interceptor. An airborne weapons platform, the F-89 was the first fighter plane designed to carry guided missiles, and the first to launch an air-to-air atomic weapon. A special modeler's section reviews available kits, including several new releases in many different scales. Plus, you'll find decal listings found only in *Detail & Scale*. By Bert Kinzey. 8 1/2 x 11, 72 pgs., over 200 b&w photos, eight pages of color photos, perfect-bound.
#05054 .... $10.95

The Detail & Scale series includes the most accurate reference guides available for scale modelers and aviation enthusiasts. Each guide includes historical summaries of developmental and operational life and close-up photos and line drawings that cover cockpit interiors, radar and avionics installations, armament and more.

U.S. Aircraft & Armament of Operation Desert Storm (Detail & Scale series vol. 40)

Now for the first time, a comprehensive, close-up look at the various combat and combat-support aircraft used by U.S. forces in the Persian Gulf War. Dozens of never-before-published photographs from the war zone show the aircraft in action, with detailed views of typical weapons loads, combat-related nose art and mission markings. A modelers' section reviews the best aircraft kits in 1/72 and 1/48 scale. By Bert Kinzey. 8 1/2 x 11, 72 pgs., over 200 b&w photos, eight pages of color photos, perfect-bound. Available March 1993.
#05056... $11.95

Look for these books at your local hobby shop.
Or call toll free, 24 hours a day 800-533-6644.

Please have your credit card ready. Fax 414-796-0126. Outside the U.S. and Canada call 414-796-8776.

Or use the enclosed order form. Include for postage and handling: U.S. add $3.00 4th class (or $4.50 UPS continental U.S. only); Canada add $5.00, other foreign countries add $10.00. Wisconsin residents add 5% sales tax to total. Canadian orders add 7% GST to total. Payable in U.S. funds. Prices and availability subject to change.

Kalmbach Publishing Co., Dept. Z063, 21027 Crossroads Circle, P.O. Box 1612, Waukesha, WI 53187-1612

Dept. Z063